ON A ROLL

ON A ROLL

A Conversation and Listening Text

Sharon Peters

Cabrillo College
Santa Cruz, California

PRENTICE HALL REGENTS, Englewood Cliffs, New Jersey 07632

Library of Congress Cataloging-in-Publication Data

Peters, Sharon.
    On a roll : a conversation and listening text / Sharon Peters.
    ISBN 0-13-155326-7
    1. English language—Textbooks for foreign speakers. 2. English
language—Conversation and phrase books. 3. Listening. I. Title.
PE1128.P4   1991
428.3′4—dc20   90-42935
                                                                  CIP

Editorial/production supervision and
   interior design: **Kala Dwarakanath**
Cover design: **Miriam Recio**
Pre-press buyer: **Ray Keating**
Manufacturing buyer: **Lori Bulwin**
Photo research: **Louise Capuano**

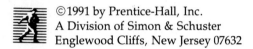

©1991 by Prentice-Hall, Inc.
A Division of Simon & Schuster
Englewood Cliffs, New Jersey 07632

Printed in the United States of America
10 9 8 7 6 5 4 3 2 1

ISBN   0-13-155326-7

Prentice-Hall International (UK) Limited, *London*
Prentice-Hall of Australia Pty. Limited, *Sydney*
Prentice-Hall Canada Inc., *Toronto*
Prentice-Hall Hispanoamericana, S.A., *Mexico*
Prentice-Hall of India Private Limited, *New Delhi*
Prentice-Hall of Japan, Inc., *Tokyo*
Simon & Schuster Asia Pte. Ltd., *Singapore*
Editora Prentice-Hall do Brasil, Ltda., *Rio de Janeiro*

*This book is dedicated to the memory of my dear friend
Mary Smith. She kept us all laughing.*

ACKNOWLEDGMENT

To all of the Cabrillo College students who gave me my ideas, to Fred Winterbottom whose creative energies helped get this project off the ground, and to Kathryn George whose competent teaching made my first hundred or so hours at the Macintosh almost fun.

PHOTO CREDITS

Contents

Preface

On a Roll was written for high-intermediate and advanced ESL/EFL students. It is meant to help prepare non-native English speakers to understand and use the rapid, reduced, idiomatic speech heard outside the classroom and the language lab.

Educational programs are varied, and so the text's use may vary accordingly. It would be appropriate as a primary text in a conversation class, a supplemental text in a combined skills class, or an individualized text to be used with script tapes in the lab or at home. *On a Roll* is both situational and contemporary.

The text is non-grammar-based, therefore, its twelve chapters may be followed in any order. A chapter may be chosen because it is relevant to what is being discussed, or because it holds interesting and useful information for the students.

Ideas for the various topics came from my students—from private and classroom discussions of situations the students found uncomfortable due to their lack of English proficiency or unfamiliarity with North American culture. We had great fun developing and using the materials for this text. I hope you find it equally useful and enjoyable.

Introduction to the Teacher

On a Roll has been designated as a listening/speaking text. It is indeed, but also much more. My belief in an integrated approach to language learning has led me to include activities that would allow your students to do some reading and writing, as well. The writing activities offer greater options because they can be used for writing or discussion. Students are asked to respond to what they have read or listened to, and so must pay close attention to the material. Writing also enables students who work independently to check their own comprehension.

Each chapter has eleven parts: the *general warm-up questions* help set the tone for disussion or study; the *pre-listening/reading questions* help students focus on specific points when they read or listen to each script; the *vocabulary* section defines words and expressions that may be new to the students. Because the intention is to help the students understand how the vocabulary is used in a specific context in the script, not all of the possible definitions are given.

The *scripts* themselves deserve special comment. They are considerably longer than traditional ESL/EFL dialogues. The short exchanges we are accustomed to serve an important function for lower-level students; the more advanced students, however, require contemporary language that is both idiomatic and useful. I view the longer scripts in this text as mini-dramas that can be segmented or used as reading passages. For the seven years that I have field-tested these materials both in the U.S. and South America, my revisions at the request of students and colleagues have always led to longer, more complex scripts.

The *post-listening/reading* questions that follow each script help the students review and respond in writing to what they have listened to or read; *vocabulary building* sentences expose students to some of the contemporary language used differently; students are also asked to create their own sentences using what they have just learned.

The *word forms* section is part of a traditional approach and often helpful for those who want to see something both familiar and useful. Because this was not intended as a grammar-based text, *word forms* is the only section that deals specifically with English syntax; the *conversation activities* allow the students to apply the new concepts to their personal experiences. This section, like the others, can be used for writing practice and/or discussion. It can also be a springboard for more detailed creative writing, discussion, and analysis.

In the *suggested role plays*, students will find discussion material relevant to their own lives. The ideas introduced are often directly related to those presented or alluded to earlier in the chapter; the *listening comprehension cloze passage* can be divided into sections, or presented as one long passage. This fairly long listening comprehension activity more closely imitates the intensity expected of our students as they advance to higher levels; the *final project* not only attempts to reinforce earlier ideas, but challenges students to apply them on their own.

Introduction to the Student

Welcome to **On a Roll**. Before you begin, I would like to explain how you can use the various parts of the chapters effectively.

General warm-up questions introduce you to the chapter; *pre-listening/reading questions* help you focus on the script; *vocabulary* enables you to understand new idioms and expressions.

Script helps you understand the speech of native speakers. The voices on the tape are those of native English speakers. Stop the tape and start again as many times as you like. Try to repeat some of the sentences as you hear them. If you don't have the tape, practice saying the script out loud with other students. You may spend several days on one tape until you have understood it. It is also helpful to listen to the script and practice it later.

Post-listening/reading questions test your memory; *vocabulary building sentences* give you opportunities to use the idioms found in the script. The *model* shows you how to invent your own sentences using these idioms. If you can, practice your new vocabulary on native speakers; ask them to use it.

Word forms give you practice in using different forms of speech; *conversation activities* enable you to think about, discuss or write down how the general topic of the chapter fits your own life; in *suggested role plays*, you will work with other students to find an ending. Others will want to hear your ending. If you work alone, you may want to use it for writing practice. What would the characters in the role play say next? Can you finish the play by yourself? Perhaps you can practice your English speaking skills with a friend.

Listening comprehension cloze passages tell you how well you can listen to and understand native English speakers. These passages are different from the scripts—there is usually just one speaker. Listen to the tape and try to fill in the blanks with the words you have just heard. You may listen more than once. If you are in a classroom, your teacher may read it to you.

Final projects give you another chance to practice oral and writing skills. Each final project is a little different from the other.

Finally, I would like to wish you lots of luck in your studies.

Sharon Peters.

ON A ROLL

1

The Potluck

General Warm-Up Questions

Do you like to study? Many people have one particular place where they like to study. Where do you usually study? Is it easy for you to study when there's music playing or when the television is on? Do you like to study alone? What kinds of things do you like to do when you've finished studying?

Who does most of the cooking in your household? Do you like to cook? Do you think you're a good cook? Do your friends think you're a good cook? When you get together with your friends and you are asked to bring something to eat, do you prepare something special, or do you pick up something at the store? Have you ever been to a potluck? When you go to a potluck, what do you like to bring?

Prelistening/Reading Study Questions

What does Fred have to study? What is Sharon making for the potluck? What should Fred bring to the potluck? Do you think that he likes to dance? Why? When will Sharon go to the party? When is it important to be on time for a party?

Vocabulary

YUCK: a common expression of dislike (Cultural note: This is an expression that is common among friends who are close to your own age and in informal situations.)

TO TAKE A BREAK: to stop doing something for a period of time, to rest

R and R: rest and relaxation; something relaxing, enjoyable (Originally a military term, R and R has become quite common in casual speech.)

POTLUCK: a meal made from whatever is available or contributed by others (Cultural note: Potlucks are quite common in the United States and do not mean that the person giving the party does not have enough money to pay for everything himself or herself. They are a way of sharing and trying different things.)

HEAVY DUTY: serious; not frivolous

TO SHOW UP: to come, to appear, to arrive

TO THROW TOGETHER: to make in a hurry, often without care (Cultural note: Some people say they "threw something together" when they worked very hard on it, but they don't want to brag or call attention to themselves so they minimize the work involved.)

FANCY: decorated; ornate; not plain, not simple

GONNA: going to (This expression is common in fast, casual speech. When you are writing, it should be written as *going to*.)

YEAH: yes (This expression is common in fast, casual speech. When you are writing, it should always be written as *yes*.)

TO KNOW WHAT SOMETHING IS LIKE: to understand, to be sympathetic to someone

YA: you (Note that the pronunciation is the same as it is for *yeah*. This expression is common in fast, casual speech. When you are writing, it should always be written as *you*.)

IT'D: it would (This pronunciation is common in fast, casual speech. When you are writing, it should be written as *it would*.)

THAT'D: that would (This pronunciation is common in fast, casual speech. When you are writing, it should be written as *that would*.)

WHADDAYA: what do you (This pronunciation is common in fast, casual speech. When you are writing, it should always be written as *what do you*.)

GOTTA: (have) got to (This pronunciation is common in fast, casual speech. When you are writing, it should always be written as *got to*.)

TO GET (it, something) OUT OF THE WAY: to finish something, to complete it; to put something aside

TO HANDLE (something or someone): to take care of, to deal with, to resolve

TO SET THINGS (SOMETHING) UP: to prepare, to organize

I'LL: I will (This pronunciation is common in fast, casual speech.)

TO LIGHTEN UP: to become less serious; to relax

Sharon: What are you gonna do this weekend?

Fred: Nothing special. I have a test to study for in math.

Sharon: Yuck. I hate math.

Fred: It's not so bad. It just takes a lot of time. I've got homework to do every night.

Sharon: I've got a chemistry class that's almost as bad. It seems like I've been living in the chem lab lately. I'm ready to take a break! How about some R and R? Speaking of R and R, did John tell you about the party he's gonna have this Saturday night?

Fred: Yeah. I'd like to go, but you know what it's like. I've got a lot of studying to do. It never seems to end.

Sharon: Aw, come on. It's Saturday night! It'd be good for you to take a break from all that heavy duty studying for a few hours.

Fred: Well, maybe I'll show up for a little while. It's a potluck, isn't it?

Sharon: Yeah, I think I might make a big fruit salad. Everyone usually likes fruit. I thought I'd just throw together some apples, oranges, bananas, and whatever else is in season or on sale.

Fred: That sounds good, but if I come I'm not going to have time to put anything fancy together, and I'm not a good cook anyway.

Sharon: No problem. The whole idea of a potluck is just to bring whatever you can. There are always a few people who have more time and are good cooks to bring main dishes and desserts.

Fred: So whaddaya think I should bring?

Sharon: The important thing is that you come, and that you bring something—anything! You could just bring a loaf of French bread or a bag of potato chips. That'd be fine.

Fred: Hmmm. A loaf of French bread or a bag of potato chips; I can handle that. Sounds pretty easy. Maybe I'll come after all. I'll bring some of my tapes, too. I've got some great music for dancing. What time does it start?

Sharon: John said something about seven o'clock, but I'll probably get there a little early. I told him I'd help set things up.

Fred: OK. If I come I'll probably be there at about 8 or 8:30. Is that too late?

Sharon: Heck no. You've only gotta worry about being right on time when someone asks you over for dinner and plans for everything to be ready at exactly the right time.

Fred: Well, if 8 or 8:30 isn't too late, I'd really like to come. I think you're right. I do need to take a break. Besides, if I go home right now, I'll still have time to get my math homework out of the way before the party. OK, why not? You're right. I do need to lighten up a little bit. I'll see ya' there.

Sharon: Great! I'm glad you've decided to come. John's parties are always a lot of fun. See ya' later.

Postlistening/Reading Questions

> Answer in complete sentences.

1. What does Fred have to study?

   _____

2. Who is having a potluck?

   _____

3. What is Sharon making for the potluck?

   _____

4. What does she think Fred should bring to the potluck?

   _____

5. Do you think that Fred likes to dance? Why? Why not?

   _____

6. Will Sharon go to the party late?

   _____

7. When is it important to be on time for a party?

   _____

Vocabulary Building Sentences

> First, underline the word or expression from the vocabulary list in the
> prelistening/reading section. Then write a new sentence, using the same word or
> expression.

MODEL: My mom gets really mad when I'm late. You <u>know what it's like</u>.

Everyone knows what it's like to be broke.

_____

1. Yuck! Green beans again? I hate them!

   _____

2. I can't take a break until I've finished cleaning my room.

_____

3. You can come over for dinner, but you'll have to take potluck.

_____

4. I didn't do anything special this weekend. I just enjoyed a little R and R.

_____

5. I can't handle being around David and Mary. Lately they're fighting all of the time.

_____

6. Can you wait while I finish doing the dishes? I want to get them out of the way before we go.

_____

7. I don't know where he is. He didn't show up for class today.

_____

8. This house looks like it was thrown together. I bet it will fall down in the next earthquake.

_____

9. I've had a toothache all week. I have to call the dentist and set up an appointment.

_____

Word Forms

Complete the following sentences with the correct word form.

fanciest   fancy   fancier

1. That rock star bought a _____ new house.

2. He has a _____ house than I do.

3. His house is as _____ as the vice president's.

4. The White House is the _____ house I've ever seen.

Conversation Activities

What do you think about potlucks? Are they a good idea? How do people from your native country entertain their friends? Do you think it is better for the person who is having the party to provide all of the food and all of the drinks? What was your favorite party, and why was it your favorite? Should people who are under 21 years of age be able to drink alcohol?

Do you think that there are many people in the United States who are worried about being on time? When is it important to be right on time in your native country?

Suggested Role-Plays

Working in groups or in pairs, prepare a dialogue to share with the class. The following topics are suggestions for you to use.

1. **Participants: Fred and his math teacher**
   Because Fred doesn't understand his math assignment, he has decided to stay and talk to his teacher after class. Your role-play could begin as follows:

   Fred: Excuse me, do you have some time to talk to me?
   Teacher: Sure, what is the problem?
   Fred: I don't understand prime factoring.
   Teacher: Can you come to my office hour at eleven o'clock?

   Finish the dialogue.

2. **Participants: Sharon, John, and John's grandparents**
   John is getting ready for a potluck with his friends when his grandparents arrive unannounced from another city.

   John: Boy, I'm sure looking forward to partying with my friends. I've been studying pretty hard lately.
   Sharon: I know what you mean. Where should I put this salad?
   John: Hey, that looks great! Just put it over there on the table. Oh, there's the doorbell. Who could it be? It's too early for any of our friends.

   Finish the dialogue.

The Potluck

3. **Participants: David and Janet**

   Janet answers the door for John, who is busy in the kitchen. She is one of the guests at the potluck. She has brought a very special casserole that has always been a favorite of her family. It is made with spinach and tofu. David hates spinach and tofu, but he doesn't want to hurt Janet's feelings.

   Janet: Hi, David! I'm glad that you could come! John's in the kitchen. Did you finish your math homework?

   David: Not quite, but I'll finish it tomorrow morning.

   Janet: I finished mine. If you need any help, give me a call. You have to eat some of the casserole I made. It's my mom's favorite recipe.

   David: Sounds great! What does it have in it?

   Janet: It has a lot of different stuff, but the main ingredients are spinach and tofu.

Finish the dialogue.

Listening Comprehension Cloze Passage

> Listen to the tape of the following passage or to your teacher. Fill in the missing words as you hear them.

Potlucks are very _____ in the United States. They give people the chance
1

to get _____ and to share food and conversation. Food is something many peo-
2

ple enjoy _____ about, and a potluck gives everyone the opportunity to
3

_____ with foods they might not have tasted _____.
4   5

When you move into a new house _____ apartment, it is common
6

to invite some friends and members of _____ family to a housewarming
7

potluck. A housewarming _____ you the chance to show your friends and
8

family _____ you live and to make them feel welcome in your new place.
9

_____ people who come to a _____ bring food to share as well
10   11

as small gifts for you to _____ in your new home. Some common housewarming
12

gifts are flowers, plants, dishtowels, _____, kitchen cutlery, utensils, table lin-
13

ens, candlesticks, or wine. The gifts are _____ usually expensive or big. If
14

your family and friends _____ that you are setting up housekeeping for the
15

_____ time, and need many things, they will often bring very
16

_____ gifts. If you have _____ many things with you from where
17   18

you lived before, the gifts you receive are _____ more decorative than
19

_____. Housewarmings are often potlucks, and offer an inexpensive, culturally
20

_____ way to have a party, show your friends and family your new house, and
21

_____ a few gifts in the bargain! If you are not _____ receiving
22   23

gifts, it is acceptable to _____ people you invite that it is not
24

_____ to bring a gift.
25

Final Project

There are many places where you can buy things that you need for your house, dorm, or apartment. In the United States, it is very common to buy things that are not new. Many times you can find what you need at garage sales or at flea markets. If you are buying dishes, silverware, pans, linens, or furniture, it is easy to see what condition they are in before you buy them. If you are buying small electrical appliances, the seller will usually let you plug them in somewhere to check them out and make sure that they work. It's fun to shop at garage sales and flea markets where you can find good bargains—it's also a lot cheaper than buying everything new.

Invent a "wish list" of all of the things you would like to buy for your room, apartment, or house if you had a lot of money. Perhaps you would like to have a king-sized heated water bed, a food processor, a rocking chair, or a new stereo. Write everything down. Now open a copy of the local newspaper to the classified ad section. Find as many of the things that are on your list as you can. You may want to look under the headings "Merchandise for Sale," "Garage Sales," "Home Furnishings," "Collectables," "Articles for Sale," "Personal Computers"—or anywhere else you might find the things you want to have. The classified section is sometimes a little different in each newspaper. How many things were you able to find? Where did you find them? Make at least two phone calls to check out something you would like to buy. Ask questions about the item listed in the paper. Write down all of the information you are given. Talk to your classmates about what you have learned.

2

After Class

General Warm-Up Questions

Read the following questions before you begin. They will help you to focus on the topic covered in this chapter.

Do you like classes that meet for two or three hours at a time? What do you think is the perfect length of time for a class period? Is it different with different subjects? A break during a class gives you some time to relax and talk to friends, but it also sometimes stops your concentration. Some people think that it's better not to take breaks during a class. Do you agree? How often should you have breaks?

When you know that you are going to have a test, how do you study? Do you study a little bit all term, or do you wait and do all of your studying at the last minute? What do you think is the best way to prepare for a test? Some teachers like to give surprise tests. You don't have time to prepare, but you also don't have time to worry. Are surprise tests a good idea? What was the most difficult subject you have studied? What subject is the easiest for you?

Prelistening/Reading Study Questions

Read the following questions before you listen to or read the dialogue. Take a few moments to think about them. They will help you understand the dialogue when you begin.

What kind of test did Fred have? What does his psychology instructor do? What time is he supposed to get out of class? Sharon gives Fred some advice. What does she think he should do? What class does Fred have right after psychology? If the teacher doesn't see Fred putting on his jacket, what does Sharon think he should do? Do you know what grade Fred got on his midterm?

Vocabulary

TO HOLD ON: to wait for someone; to slow down or pause for a moment

A SEC: a second; a very short period of time (This expression is common in fast, casual speech. When you are writing, it should always be written as a second.)

D'YA: do you (This is common in fast, casual speech. When you are writing, these words should always be written as *do you*.)

TO KEEP UP (WITH THE JONESES): to continue; to go at the same speed as others

YA: you (Note that the pronunciation is the same as it is for *yeah*. This pronunciation is common in fast, casual speech. When you are writing, it should always be written as *you*.)

MIDTERM: a test (examination) that is usually given in the middle of the semester or quarter

'EM: them (This expression is common in fast, casual speech. When you are writing, it should be written as *them*.)

PRETTY SURE: reasonably certain of something

WANNA: want to (This expression is common in fast, casual speech. When you are writing, it should be written as *want to*.)

TO ACE: (a test or a course): to do very well; to get an excellent grade (from the highest card in a deck—the ace)

TEN TO: ten minutes before the hour

TO BE ON A ROLL: to have things going smoothly; to build up momentum; to be moving physically or mentally

PSYCH: abbreviation for psychology; the science of mind and behavior

TO GET SOMEWHERE: to accomplish something, to be successful

TO GRIPE: to express pain, unhappiness, or displeasure

POLITE: courteous, well-mannered, considerate to others

BACK-TO-BACK: to have more than one thing to do with little or no time in between

TO PACK UP: to put things away; to get ready to go

DENSE: thick, solid; crowded (population); slow to understand (a person)

TO STARE: to look at steadily without looking away

TO CATCH ON: to understand what's happening, to comprehend suddenly

TO SHIFT AROUND: to change positions; not to sit still in your seat

TO GIVE SOMETHING A TRY: to try something; to make an attempt at a job, a lesson, and so on

BRAINSTORM: a very good idea; usually an idea that comes like a storm—without warning or time to prepare for it

AFTER CLASS

Sharon: Hey, Fred, hold on a sec! Are you headed for class?

Fred: Yeah. I have psych at 10.

Sharon: D'ya like it?

Fred: It's not bad, but there's a lot of reading to do. Sometimes it's hard to keep up.

Sharon: Have ya' had any tests yet?

Fred: Yeah, we had a midterm last week.

Sharon: How'd ya' do on it?

Fred: I don't know yet. The teacher said that we'll get 'em back today. I'm pretty sure I did OK, but sometimes it's really hard to tell.

Sharon: Well, I'll meet you after class in the cafeteria. I'll wait for you. I wanna know how you did.

Fred: OK. See ya' after class. Yeah, I studied pretty hard. I think I did OK. I don't know why I'm so worried. Maybe I aced it!

(Later, in the cafeteria)

Sharon: Oh, hi Fred! I didn't know whether to save you a place or not. I've been waiting for quite a while. I thought you'd be here sooner.

Fred: Our psych teacher always keeps us in class until eleven o'clock exactly. She's a great teacher, but she never lets us out on time.

Sharon: Doesn't she know that you're supposed to get out at ten to?

Fred: I guess so, but once she's on a roll, she won't stop lecturing. I don't think she ever looks at the clock. She just keeps talking.

Sharon: Don't the students gripe about it? I think I would say something.

Fred: Nah, everyone's too polite, I guess. We all just sit there quietly and wait for her to finish.

Sharon: What if you have another class back-to-back with psychology? Wouldn't you be late for your next class all the time?

Fred: I guess so, I guess I'm lucky. I don't have another class right after, but I know some students who do.

Sharon: Have you tried talking to the teacher?

Fred: Yeah. I know that some of my friends have. Maybe I should talk to her, too.

Sharon: What did the teacher do when your friends talked to her? Did your friends get somewhere?

Fred: Nah, not really. After they talked to her, she let us out on time for a few days, and then she forgot and started keeping us until eleven o'clock again. It's really frustrating.

Sharon: If you're sure that some of the students have tried to talk to her and she still keeps you late, why don't you just try packing up at ten to eleven?

Fred: What do you mean?

Sharon: You know, just start quietly putting your books in your backpack, putting your pencil away, and putting on your jacket.

Fred: That might work. But do you think that she'll notice? Sometimes she seems pretty dense.

Sharon: Well, if that fails, start staring at the clock and shift around in your seat. Teachers usually catch on when the students start moving around a little.

Fred: All right, I think I'll give it a try.

Sharon: Tell your classmates to do the same thing. It usually works better if there's more than one student doing it. Hey, I forgot to ask, how did you do on your midterm?

Fred: The midterm? I'd rather not talk about it.

Sharon: Oh, no! That bad, huh? Well, I've got a brainstorm. Let's go get some lunch. I'm hungry.

Postlistening/Reading Questions

Answer in complete sentences.

1. What kind of test did Fred have?

   _____

2. What does Fred's psychology instructor do?

   _____

3. What time is Fred supposed to get out of class?

_____

4. What does Sharon think Fred should do first?

_____

5. What class does Fred have right after psychology?

_____

6. If the teacher doesn't see Fred putting on his jacket, what does Sharon think he should do?

_____

7. What grade did Fred get on his midterm?

_____

Vocabulary Building Sentences

> First, underline the word or expression from the vocabulary list in the prelistening/reading section. Then write a new sentence, using the same word or expression. Follow the model.

MODEL: I just had a brainstorm! Let's go to the mountains this weekend.

That was a real brainstorm. I'm glad you thought about going to the movies.

1. Hold on a sec! I forgot my books, and I have to go back to the classroom.

_____

2. I'm headed for the snack bar. Do you want to come with me?

_____

3. Did you ace that last class?

_____

4. My bus leaves at five to eight every morning.

_____

5. My neighbors bought a new car because they're trying to keep up with the Joneses.

_____

6. I'd like to come with you, but I'm going to keep studying. I'm finally beginning to understand this. I'm on a roll, and I don't want to stop.

_____

7. John is exhausted. He just had two midterms back-to-back.

_____

8. If my husband and I have one more fight, I'm going to pack up and get out.

_____

9. I tried to call my brother, but he won't talk to me. I didn't get anywhere with him because he's so mad at me that he won't even listen.

_____

10. Don't say anything to David about the surprise party. I don't want him to catch on.

_____

11. I like to take my son to church with me, but he shifts around too much.

_____

12. Wait up a minute! I'll go with you.

_____

Word Forms

> Complete the following sentences with the correct word form.

complaint   complainer   complains

1. My father _____ every time I am five minutes late.

2. Many stores have a _____ department.

3. My little brother is a constant _____.

polite   impolite   politely

1. If you ask me _____, I will give you more milk.

2. She is so _____ that she always smiles and says hello.

3. It is very _____ to interrupt when someone is talking.

stare   staring

1. That woman has been _____ at you for an hour. Do you know her?

2. In many cultures, it's not polite to _____ at someone.

Conversation Activities

> Working in groups, discuss the following:

What would you do if your teacher regularly kept you in class late? Do you think what Sharon suggested was fair? In your native country, what do the students do when the teacher keeps them late? What would you do if you had to leave the classroom before the class was finished? Are the students in your native country punished if they do something the teacher thinks is not right? Do you think that teachers have the right to punish students?

Suggested Role-Plays

> Working in groups or in pairs, prepare a dialogue to share with the class. The following topics are suggestions for you to use.

1. **Participants: Fred and his psychology teacher**
   Fred has decided to stay and talk to his teacher about the class.

   Fred: Hi, Dr. Nelson. Can I talk with you for a minute?
   Dr. Nelson: Sure. Do you have another class right now?
   Fred: No, I don't.
   Dr. Nelson: Why don't you just come with me to my office, and we can talk there.
   Fred: OK, that's fine.
   Dr. Nelson: Are you having problems with the class?

   Finish the dialogue.

2. **Participants: Sharon, Janet, David, and Bruce**
   Sharon and Janet are in the cafeteria waiting for Fred. They are all worried about their midterms.

   Janet: How many midterms do you have coming up, Sharon?
   Sharon: I have two this week and two next week. How about you?
   Janet: I have three.

Sharon: Are they all this week?

Janet: Nope. They're all next week. Chemistry's the only one I'm really worried about.

Sharon: Yuck! I'm glad that I decided to wait and take chemistry next semester.

Janet: It's the toughest. I need to find some people to study with. If we can get a group together, it will be easier. You know the old saying, "Misery loves company." Hey! There are David and Bruce! They're both good chemistry students, and they're both in my class. Hey, David! Bruce! Will you guys come over here for a minute?

Finish the dialogue.

Listening Comprehension Cloze Passage

> Listen to the tape of the following passage or to your teacher. Fill in the missing words as you hear them.

Dear Mom and Dad:

Well, you _____ be pleased to hear that I got through my
1

midterms again without any real _____ . I was worried about
2

chemistry—you know that it has _____ been
3

_____ for me. When I was in high school, I always had to work
4

very _____ to get good grades in math and science. It is a lot
5

_____ to study science here in college. The teachers
6

_____ much more of us. They don't _____ us
7   8

really hard, or get mad at us when we don't _____
9

_____ assignments on time. We must be _____
10   11

for our own actions. If we _____ get our work in on time, we
12

just don't get a good grade. I have to push _____ a lot here.
13

There is a tutorial center _____ we can all _____
14   15

to get help, and the teachers are all _____ to help us, but
16

sometimes I am _____ to ask for help. My friend Sharon is
17

_____ with me to talk to someone in the tutorial
18

_____ tomorrow.
        19

    I _____ love school, and I know that I will have to
             20

_____ to work very hard in all of my classes. Sometimes I get
        21

_____ lonely, and I think about all of you and how
        22

_____ I miss you. I am starting to make some
        23

_____ friends who are _____ me a lot. Please
        24   25

write back to me soon, and tell everyone _____ to write! I love
                                            26

to get _____. Give everyone my love and tell them that I
            27

_____ them.
        28

    I'll write again soon.

                                                                Love,

                                                                Janet

Final Project

It is not enough to know how to read, write, and speak a new language. As you learn the vocabulary and the grammar of a language, you must learn where and when to use the different styles of speech. If you met the president of the United States, you would probably not say, "Hey, how ya' doin?" But you might say that to a close friend. The situation is the same when you are writing. Formal school papers are written differently than letters, and personal letters are written differently than business letters. Personal letters to different people are written differently.

Think about the letter Janet wrote to her parents.
1. Write a letter to a grandparent, or another respected older person. Describe a problem you are having and tell the person how you think you can solve the problem.
2. Write a letter to your very best friend. Describe a problem and tell your friend how you think you can solve the problem.
3. Write a letter to a grandparent, or another respected older person. Tell the person about the great party you went to at John's last Saturday night.
4. Write a letter to your very best friend. Tell your friend about the great party you went to at John's last Saturday night.

Thursday Night at the Supermarket

General Warm-Up Questions

Read the following questions before you begin. They will help you to focus on the topic covered in this chapter.

Do you like to go grocery shopping? If you don't like to grocery shop, why don't you? Is it easier for you to shop when you have made a list of what you need? What happens when you have not made a list? When you go shopping, do you go by yourself?

People in the United States eat a lot of fast foods. Is the same thing happening in other countries? What kinds of fast foods do you like? How do you feel about tasting foods you have never eaten before? Do you like to eat the same things all of the time? Many people eat different things for dinner, but they often have the same things for breakfast every morning. Do you? Why do you think this is true? If you had to choose one kind of food that you would have to eat every day for the rest of your life, what would it be?

Prelistening/Reading Study Questions

Read the following questions before you listen to or read the dialogue. Take a few moments to think about them. They will help you understand the dialogue when you begin.

What did Fred plan to buy at the grocery store? How many shopping carts did Fred and Sharon use? Where does the store keep the butter? Is there a specific reason why Fred doesn't like Diet Pepsi®? What does Sharon think about Brussels sprouts? Where does Fred usually shop? What are Fred and Sharon going to do on Friday?

Vocabulary

TO PICK SOMEONE OR SOMETHING UP: to take on or away; to receive, to get; to pay for someone else (to pick up the check)

THE PITS: unpleasant; boring; something you don't like to do (This expression is common only in casual, informal speech among friends who are close to the same age.)

WANNA: want to (This expression is common in fast, casual speech. When you are writing, it should be written as *want to*.)

TO STOCK UP: to get a lot of something at one time

GROCERIES: meats, produce, dairy products, and household items

SHOPPING CART: a metal basket with wheels for carrying groceries

A PURIST: someone who believes everything should be in its pure or natural form

PERK: a bonus; something good that is unexpected (This term is commonly used to describe extra employee benefits.)

DAIRY CASE: a glass case where dairy products are kept

TO BE ON SALE: to be at a lower price; to be cheaper than usual

Thursday Night at the Supermarket

NEVER TOUCH THE STUFF: don't eat or drink something

TO CHECK OUT: to look at something; to leave (check out of a hotel or motel; to pay for your purchases at a cashier's counter)

TO CHECK A LIST: to refer to a piece of paper where you have written down the things you need

VEGGIES: vegetables

MUNCHIES: any small things (like fruit, potato chips, cookies) that are good to eat (to munch on); not a full meal; snacks

YUCK: a common expression of dislike (Cultural note: This is an expression that is common in informal situations among friends who are close to the same age.)

STINKY: something that is offensive, or that doesn't smell good (This expression is used in casual speech among people of the same age.)

'EM: them (This expression is common in fast, casual speech. When you are writing, it should be written as *them*.)

TO GET DOWN TO: to get to the heart (of something); to the important part (This expression is common in many situations and among people of different age groups—for example, "Let's get down to business.")

TO FIX: to make or prepare (food); to repair

EXPENSIVE: costing a lot of money; high in price; the opposite of *cheap*

ADDITIVES: chemicals and coloring added to food

HOSTESS TWINKIES®:   a brand name for small, packaged cakes

HOPELESS: without hope; impossible to change or solve

TO CHILL OUT: to relax; to calm down; to become less serious (This expression is common only in casual, informal speech among friends who are close to the same age.)

TO GO UP (in price):   to become more expensive

TO SLAVE OVER A HOT STOVE: to work hard cooking something

TO STRETCH SOMETHING OUT: to add other things so that something will last longer, go farther, or feed more people

VEGETARIAN: a person who does not eat meat

TO MIX AND MATCH: to try different combinations; to put things together

CHECKOUT STAND: the counter in a store where you pay for the things that you want to buy

FOOD STAMPS: stamps that are issued by the Federal government to low-income people. Food stamps are coupons that can be used instead of money to buy food.

EXPRESS LINE: a faster checkout stand where you can pay for your purchases if you have no more than a certain number of items

TO GIVE SOMEONE A LIFT: to give someone a ride in a car

RUNNING (SOMEONE) AROUND: to drive someone where he or she needs to go (This expression is common in casual speech.)

TO HIT IT (RIGHT ON THE HEAD): to arrive at a specific time or place; to concentrate or focus on something; to get something done

WHOA: wait a minute (This is common only in casual speech.)

TO PUT OFF (doing something): to wait to do something; to postpone

TO GIVE SOMEONE A CALL: to call someone on the telephone

TO PASS: to choose not to do something; to let something go by

THURSDAY NIGHT AT THE SUPERMARKET

Sharon: I'm glad you could pick me up and take me to the grocery store. I hate to carry a lot of stuff on the bus. It's the pits.

Fred: That's OK. I like the company. I hate to shop alone. Anyway, they're having a sale on laundry soap and yogurt. I wanna stock up.

(In the store)

Sharon: Do you need a shopping cart?

Fred: I don't have whole lot to buy. Why don't we put everything together into one cart?

Sharon: OK. I haven't shopped here in a while. Do you know where they keep the butter?

Fred: Sure. It's way in the back of the store in the dairy case.

Sharon: Great, thanks. Hey! Check out this fancy display. They sure want us to buy Diet Pepsi®, don't they?

Fred: Yuck. I never touch the stuff. It's all chemicals.

Sharon: Aw, Fred, you're such a purist! Oh, here's the butter. All right! It's on sale. That's a perk. And here's the milk. Now, let's see . . . what else do I need? Let me check my list. My memory's getting worse and worse every day. I've got to write everything down. My list has got to be here somewhere. Don't tell me I left it at home! Oh great, here it is. Let's see now . . . I need some veggies, some hamburger, and some munchies. This lettuce looks pretty good, and it's cheap.

Fred: Yuck. Most of these vegetables look pretty bad. I'll bet they were all sprayed with chemicals. I'll just get some garlic and some Brussels sprouts.

Sharon: Bleah! I hate Brussels sprouts. Do you really like those stinky little cabbages?

Fred: Sure! You just have to know how to cook 'em. I fix them in a cheese sauce with Dijon-style mustard and herbs. They're great.

Sharon: What kind of cheese do you use, American?

Fred: Are you kidding? I don't call that cheese. I buy good jack, Swiss, or cheddar cheese at the organic food store where they don't use any food coloring or chemicals. Don't you shop at the natural foods store?

Sharon: I've heard that the stuff there is pretty expensive.

Fred: It's no more expensive than here, and best of all, it's all organic.

Sharon: Do you really believe all that you hear about additives? I think you worry too much. We're all going to die sometime. Now. I need to get down to the most important things on my list. Where are the Hostess Twinkies®?

Fred: You're hopeless. Don't you know what's in Hostess Twinkies®?

Sharon: Sure I do, cake and filling and sugar and good sweet stuff. They're great to eat in front of the TV late at night. Sometimes I carry a package of Twinkies® in my purse to eat when I need some energy in a hurry.

Fred: Do you wanna lose all of your teeth? Why don't you grab a piece of fruit or some frozen yogurt?

Sharon: Hey, chill out. You're too serious. Ah, here's the meat section. I need a couple of pounds of hamburger. I can't believe how much beef has gone up in the last few months. Maybe I'll just buy one pound and stretch it out.

Fred: That's one of the reasons that I became a vegetarian.

Sharon: What do you fix instead of meat?

Fred: I get protein from lots of other foods. I eat brown rice, beans, tofu, and nuts. You have to mix and match to get a good protein combination. It takes a lot of practice, but it's sure worth the trouble. You don't put all those chemicals in your system.

Sharon: Sounds like too much trouble to me. I need things that don't take long to cook. I don't mind making a salad or something like that, but I hate to slave over a hot stove when I could be out having a good time. Now, let's see. What else do I need? I have butter, milk, a pound of hamburger, and some Twinkies®. I still need some chocolate chips, flour, and sugar.

Fred: The chocolate chips, flour, and sugar are just one or two aisles over from the paper products and laundry soap. I'll take the cart and meet you at the checkout stand.

(At the checkout stand)

Fred: Whoa! Look at the long line of people. I guess we should've come earlier before everyone got off work. We hit it right at five o'clock.

Sharon: You're right. That wasn't very bright, was it? How many items do we have? If we have 10 or less, the sign says we can go through the express lane.

Fred: That's a good idea. Hey, they take Food Stamps here, don't they?

Sharon: Of course. Almost every grocery store takes Food Stamps.

Fred: Great!

Sharon: Thanks a lot for taking me to the store. I sure appreciate it.

Fred: No problem. Hey, by the way, I'm going to the laundromat tomorrow morning. If you have laundry to do, I can give you a lift. Even if you don't have laundry to do, I'd sure like the company.

Sharon: That's a great idea! I've been putting off washing clothes. How about if you give me a call in the morning right before you leave your house, so I can be ready to go.

Fred: OK, great! See ya' tomorrow.

Sharon: 'Bye, and thanks again for running me to the store. Why don't you come on in and have dinner with me? I'm making all of your favorite things—hamburgers, fries, and Hostess Twinkies!

Fred: It's thoughtful of you to ask, but you'll understand if I pass on this one.

Sharon: Sure. Next time I'll make a big salad and Brussels sprouts, I promise. Thanks for offering to take me to the laundromat tomorrow. Se ya' in the morning.

Fred: OK. 'Bye for now.

Postlistening/Reading Questions

> Answer in complete sentences.

1. What did Fred plan to buy at the grocery store?

   _____

2. How many shopping carts did Fred and Sharon use? Why?

   _____

3. Where is the butter kept in the store?

   _____

4. Why doesn't Fred like Diet Pepsi?

   _____

5. What does Sharon think about Brussels sprouts?

   _____

6. Where does Fred usually shop?

   _____

7. What are Fred and Sharon going to do on Friday morning?

   _____

Vocabulary Building Sentences

> First, underline the word or expression from the vocabulary list in the prelistening/reading section. Then write a new sentence, using the same word or expression. Follow the model.

MODEL: She <u>ran</u> her brother <u>around</u> all day. He was looking for just the right shirt for the wedding.

I ran around all weekend looking for a new couch.

1. He picks up languages easily.

   _____

2. I like to stock up on toothpaste so I don't run out.

   _____

3. The last guest checked out of the hotel this morning.

   _____

4. I have to check my list to see if I've bought all of my books.

   _____

5. If coffee keeps going up, I'm going to start drinking tea.

   _____

6. My rent just went up, so I'll have to stretch out my money to make it through the month.

   _____

7. My father gave me a lift to school today.

   _____

8. My daughter has been putting off going to the dentist.

   _____

9. We need to get down to business. I don't have a lot of time.

   _____

10. I gave my brother a lift last night because his car was out of gas.

    _____

11. My mother used to slave over a hot stove for two hours every evening.

_____

12. I have to pass on your invitation. I have to baby-sit tonight.

_____

13. I've been trying to teach my dog not to bark all the time, but I think that it's hopeless.

_____

Word Forms

Complete the following sentences with the correct word form.

inexpensive   expensively   expensive

1. My sister buys designer clothes. She dresses very _____.

2. I shop for bargains. My clothes are usually _____.

3. Prince Charles's wedding to Princess Diana was much more

_____ than mine was.

Conversation Activities

Working in groups, discuss the following:

Some people like to shop in small, neighborhood stores, and other people like to shop in large supermarkets. Which is better? Is it always better? It seems that groceries are getting more and more expensive every time you go to the store. What are some of the reasons this is true? Where is the most expensive place to shop in your neighborhood?

A lot of food has chemicals and additives. What do you think about this? What are some of the reasons food manufacturers use chemicals and additives in their products? What foods do you know about that have additives? Why is it important to read the labels on the food you buy? What influences what kind or brand of food you buy? What kind of an influence does television advertising have?

Many people in the United States spend a lot of money on their pets. What do you think about all of the different kinds of dog and cat food that is sold in stores in the U.S.?

Suggested Role-Plays

Working in groups or in pairs, prepare a dialogue to share with the class. The following topics are suggestions for you to use.

1. **Participants: Fred and his older brother, Jeff**
   Jeff comes over to his brother's house and hears Fred talking on the phone to Sharon. Now he knows that Fred and Sharon are going to the laundromat in the morning. Jeff hates to do laundry, so he tries to talk his brother into washing his laundry, too.

   Jeff: Hey, Fred. How's it going'? I haven't seen you in a while. How've you been, little brother?

   Fred: OK. I'm trying to get everything done before the weekend so I'll have plenty of time to study for my midterms.

   Jeff: Boy! I know what you mean! I've a lot of stuff to do, too! Hey, I couldn't help overhearing your conversation with Sharon. What's this about the laundromat tomorrow morning?

   Finish the dialogue.

2. **Participants: Janet and a stranger in the supermarket**
   Janet is shopping at the grocery store by herself. She is buying some laundry soap when a very interesting man starts asking her questions.

   Stranger: Boy. These labels are very confusing. One says use hot water, one says use cold water, one says it makes your clothes whiter, one says it makes your clothes softer. I don't understand any of this stuff.

   Janet: Yes. I know it's confusing. It's a problem for me, too.

   Stranger: Maybe you can give me some advice. I just moved into my own apartment, and this is the first time I've had to do my own laundry. What kind of soap powder would you recommend?

   Janet: Gee, I don't know. I usually use a liquid laundry soap.

   Stranger: Oh? Why is that? Excuse me. I'm not being very polite. My name is David. I should have introduced myself earlier.

   Janet: My name's Janet.

   Stranger: So, Janet. Do you shop here often?

   Finish the dialogue.

3. **Participants: David and his little sister Donna (and possibly David's girlfriend)**
   David has made a very special date for Saturday night, but he forgot that he promised his little sister Donna that he would go to her school to watch her play in the basketball game on Saturday night.

Donna: Hi, David!

David: Hey, kid! How's it goin'?

Donna: Great! I've been down at the gym all morning shooting baskets. I don't want to make any mistakes out there on the court tonight.

David: Tonight! What's so special about tonight?

Finish the dialogue.

Listening Comprehension Cloze Passage

> Listen to the tape of the following passage or to your teacher. Fill in the missing words as you hear them.

It is not unusual to have a _____ conversation in a grocery store
                              1

_____ someone you have not met before. Generally, it is a _____
        2   3

place to make new friends. _____ stores are brightly lighted, there are a lot of
                                        4

other people around, and the atmosphere is _____ and casual. If you see some-
                                                        5

one who looks _____, you can start a conversation about _____
                        6   7

you are buying, about where something is in the store, or about what fruit and

_____ look the best. It takes a _____ detective work, but some-
        8   9

times you can _____ _____ quite a bit about someone by the food
                    10   11

he or she eats. This is how Sharon _____ how she met her new boyfriend at the
                                            12

supermarket.

_____ first thing I did was to get a little _____ up. I didn't
        13   14

wear _____ and an old sweatshirt—I wore a nice skirt and blouse. I also
            15

_____ my hair differently because it seems _____ every time I go
        16   17

to the store _____ like a slob, I always _____ _____
                    18   19   20

someone I know or would like to know. This time I was prepared.

_____ 21 _____, it's easy to find out about a man from what's in his grocery

_____ 22 _____. If there are a lot of _____ 23 _____ dinners, and foods that don't

_____ 24 _____ to be cooked, the man probably doesn't like to cook or

_____ 25 _____ have time to cook. If there are fresh vegetables, meats, and grains, he

probably cooks _____ 26 _____ he has to cook or likes to cook. If there is

_____ 27 _____ food and disposable _____ 28 _____ in the shopping cart, he's

_____ 29 _____ got a wife and a baby at home. Sometimes I can _____ 30 _____ tell if

the man lives alone or with _____ 31 _____ people from what he has in his

_____ 32 _____ cart. If he buys just one steak, or one _____ 33 _____ of fish, and

very small sizes of everything else, there is a good _____ 34 _____ that he lives alone and

cooks for _____ 35 _____. I can also tell if we have anything in _____ 36 _____. If he

is buying all natural stuff and no _____ 37 _____ food, we probably wouldn't get along,

because I love junk food.

I _____ 38 _____ my new boyfriend in the produce _____ 39 _____. I was look-

ing at the cantaloupes and he was _____ 40 _____ next to me putting some peaches into

a bag in his shopping cart. He looked pretty _____ 41 _____, so I thought I would start

a _____ 42 _____. I asked him if he _____ 43 _____ how to tell if a cantaloupe was

ripe. He came over to me and _____ 44 _____. He said, "First pick up the melon

_____ 45 _____ see if it smells sweet and fresh. Then look at the mesh that

_____ 46 _____ the skin of the melon. It _____ 47 _____ look white and thick." When

I asked him how he knew so much about melons, he said his _____ 48 _____ was the

produce manager for that store! Imagine that! Well, we _____ 49 _____

_____ 50 _____ for a few more minutes; then we introduced _____ 51 _____. We

found out that we both go to the same school, _____ 52 _____. He had the same classes

last semester that I'm _____ 53 _____ with this semester! Then he offered to

Thursday Night at the Supermarket

_____ me some of his old notes and books. We agreed to _____ for
                54   55

coffee the next morning in the student center. _____ was six
                                                                        56

_____ ago, and we are still going out with each other. You _____
        57   58

know who you can meet when you're shopping at the _____.
                                                                                  59

Final Project

There is a lot of debate about when you should go grocery shopping. If you go when you are hungry, you might buy much more than you need. If you go when you aren't hungry, you will come home with less than what you need. One of the best ways to shop seems to be to prepare in advance by making a list of what you need and stick with the list.

Plan a menu for one week. Write a list of all of the food you would eat for breakfast, lunch, dinner, and snacks for one week. Based on the menu you have written, write a shopping list of what you would need to buy when you went to the store to shop for your one week's groceries. Check the prices of the items you would need, and write them down on your list.

After you have written down your menus, your grocery list, and prices, answer the following questions: How much do you usually spend on groceries each week? Do you eat in restaurants a lot? Do you eat at school? How much money do you usually spend each week eating out? When you go out to eat, do you usually go out for dinner? For lunch? For breakfast? For dessert? In the town where you live, what restaurant or store has the best dessert? What is it? Is it expensive?

4

The Laundromat

General Warm-Up Questions

Read the following questions before you begin. They will help you to focus on the topic covered in this chapter.

Many people use public transportation, but others do not. What are some of the advantages of using public transportation? If you live in a city with a good public transportation system, is a car still important? Is the public transportation system in your city good? Do you use public transportation every day? What do you think of the idea of buying a car together with a friend and sharing it? If you could choose any way to travel, how would you travel?

Some things are more difficult to do if you don't have a car. If you don't have a car, and you don't have a washing machine, how do you do your laundry? If you go to a laundromat, can you do other things while your clothes are washing? What are some other things that you can do?

Prelistening/Reading Study Questions

Read the following questions before you listen to or read the dialogue. Take a few moments to think about them. They will help you understand the dialogue when you begin.

How many loads of wash does Fred have to do? Why does Sharon put off doing her laundry? Why doesn't Fred have to divide his clothes into separate piles? Does a Big Boy hold more than a regular washing machine? How much does it hold? Why doesn't Sharon want to use the change machine? What does she buy for Fred at the deli? They plan to go out to lunch on Saturday. Why does Fred think that Sharon should pay for lunch?

Vocabulary

TO GIVE SOMEONE A LIFT: to give someone a ride in a car

A LOAD: the quantity of clothes, towels, and so on that you put into a washing machine or dryer

TO GET DOWN TO NOTHING: to have nothing left that is clean to wear; to have nothing left to eat; to have no money left to spend

TO GET THROUGH: to finish; to complete

TO PICK (SOMEONE OR SOMETHING) UP: to give someone a ride; to accompany someone; to get something for someone

TO BE USED TO: to be accustomed to something

TO PUT OFF (doing something):   to avoid; to postpone

TO END UP DOING SOMETHING: to do something you did not plan (or want) to do

A LOTTA STUFF: a lot of stuff; lots of possessions; many things. (This expression is common only in casual, informal speech.)

The Laundromat

YA': you (Note that the pronunciation is the same as it is for *yeah*. This expression is common in fast, casual speech. When you are writing, it should always be written as *you*.)

THAT'D: that would (This pronunciation is common in fast, casual speech. When you are writing, it should be written as *that would*.)

ALL THAT JAZZ: and everything else

A GOOD DEAL: a good price or low price for something you buy

FADED: no longer bright and clear; old-looking

A COUPLE OF BUCKS: a few dollars

A RIP-OFF: a bad deal; a high price for something that should be less expensive

NAH: no (This expression is common in fast, casual speech. When you are writing, it should be written as *no*.)

YUP: yes (This is common in fast, casual speech. When you are writing, it should be written as *yes*.)

ORGANIC: natural, produced without chemicals or additives

A MONSTER: a large machine

TO BREAK A DOLLAR BILL: to make change; to spend part of

A REFUND: money returned to you

DELI: a delicatessen, a store that sells prepared food like sandwiches and salads

TO KEEP AN EYE ON: to watch

TO GET (SOMETHING) OUT OF THE WAY: to finish something; to work on it to bring it closer to completion

TO BE OUT OF LINE: to do or say something that is inappropriate or wrong

TO GET SOMETHING OVER WITH: to finish something that you don't want to do

OUTRAGEOUS: something that is either very good or very bad

A PIECE OF CAKE: it's easy

TO GET CARRIED AWAY: to do more or spend more than you had planned

PERMANENT DAMAGE: harm that is impossible to fix; harm that is beyond repair

THE PITS: unpleasant; boring; something you don't like to do (This expression is common only in casual, informal speech among friends who are close to the same age.)

TO BREAK EVEN: to make as much money as you spend; to neither lose nor win something; to end up with the same amount you started with

TO TOSS SOMETHING OUT: to throw something away

TO BE WORTH SAVING: to be something that still has some value; to be something that you should not throw away

EASY COME, EASY GO: something you don't work hard to get is easy to spend or lose

Sharon: Hey, thanks for giving me a lift to the laundromat!

Fred: No problem. I have a couple of loads to do myself. Say, you've got a lotta stuff there.

Sharon: Yeah. I always put off doing my laundry because I don't have a car. When I get down to nothing, I usually end up washing a few things out by hand in the kitchen sink and hanging them up to dry in the bathroom. I hate that almost as much as going to the laundromat.

Fred: I have a car, but I still put it off. I just hate doing laundry. At least it won't be too bad today. I'll have someone to talk to while I sit around and wait for the stuff to finish in the machines.

Sharon: That's true. Now, aren't you glad you picked me up? I promise I'll keep talking the whole time.

Fred: Thanks a lot. Well, here we are. Now the fun begins. Do you want me to help ya' get all that stuff out of the car?

Sharon: Nah, that's OK. I'm used to it. Go in and get started. I'll meet you inside.

(Inside the laundromat)

Fred: Hey, it's not crowded today. We should be able to get through pretty fast. I've only got about three loads to do. I suppose I should separate them into piles of white clothes, dark clothes, and all that jazz, but I usually just throw them all into a Big Boy.

Sharon: You mean one of those giant washing machines in the back? I've never used one.

Fred: They're a good deal if you've got a lot of clothes to wash. I can throw mine all in together because my clothes are so old and faded that it doesn't matter if I wash my blue jeans with white sheets any more.

Sharon: I guess I can wash all of my things in a Big Boy, too. I hope I remembered to bring enough change. How many quarters do these monsters take?

Fred: They usually take a couple of bucks . . . maybe a little more.

Sharon: Boy, what a rip-off.

Fred: Not really. The big machine holds about three times as many clothes as the regular machine does.

Sharon: I've got five quarters and three singles. Can you break a dollar bill?

Fred: I've got just enough quarters to do my laundry. Why don't you use the change machine?

Sharon: The change machine always eats my money. The owners of the laundromat are supposed to give refunds, but you've got to find them first.

Fred: Why don't you go next door to the deli? I'll bet they'll give you change.

Sharon: That's not a bad idea. Keep an eye on my stuff, will ya?

Fred: Sure. I'm going to see if there is a magazine to read around here that isn't four years old. I should have brought my psychology book with me. I could have gotten some of my homework out of the way.

Sharon: I'll only be a minute. D'ya' want anything from the deli?

Fred: As a matter of fact, I'd really like some juice. I think they've got some unfiltered apple juice that doesn't have any chemicals in it. Just a minute, I'll give you some money.

Sharon: No way. I'll buy it for you. It's the least I can do in exchange for the ride down here.

Fred: OK, thanks. That's really nice of you. See you in a minute. I'm not going anywhere.

(A few minutes later)

Fred: Did you get the change you needed?

Sharon: Yup. It was a piece of cake. They were really nice. Here's your apple juice. I hope it's the kind you wanted. The woman in the deli said it was organic. I'm going to have to go back to that place to eat one of these days. The food looked pretty good, and the prices weren't out of line. I can't eat at home for much less.

Fred: Yeah. It's one of my favorite places. They've got some outrageous salads and lots of good cheeses. Maybe we could come down for lunch next Saturday.

Sharon: That sounds good. Have you started your wash yet?

Fred: Nope. I was waiting for you.

Sharon: Well, I guess we might as well get this over with. Nobody's going to come around and do it for us.

Fred: OK. I'll take this machine, and you take the one next to it. Say, aren't you putting in a lot of soap? That Big Boy doesn't take much.

Sharon: Oops! I guess I got carried away. At least a little too much soap can't cause any permanent damage. I sure can't afford to buy new clothes. My rent just went up.

Fred: Oh wow, that's the pits. Everything's goin' up—food, gasoline, postage, telephone bills, everything. I've still got some books to buy for this semester. I'll be lucky to break even this month. I might have to ask my big brother to lend me some money. I hate to borrow from anyone.

Sharon: I know what you mean, but sometimes you have no choice.

Fred: What's that on the counter next to your laundry basket? It looks like an old pair of jeans you forgot to put in the washer.

Sharon: Nah. I didn't put them in the washer because I've decided to toss them out. Look at them. They're so old that they're falling apart. They aren't worth saving. Hey, look! I just found a 10 dollar bill in the pocket!

Fred: Hey! That's great. It was worth it to check in the pockets before you tossed them. You know what that means—you can afford to pay for our lunch next Saturday. You did say that you were buying, didn't you?

Sharon: Next Saturday? Lunch? Oh well, easy come, easy go.

Postlistening/Reading Questions

> Answer in complete sentences.

1. How many loads of wash does Fred have to do?

   _____

2. Why does Sharon put off doing her laundry?

   _____

3. Why does Fred think they should be able to wash their clothes quickly?

   _____

4. Why doesn't Fred have to divide his clothes into separate piles?

   _____

5. How much more laundry does a Big Boy hold than a regular washing machine?

   _____

6. Why doesn't Sharon want to use the change machine?

   _____

7. What does Sharon buy Fred at the deli?

   _____

8. Why does Fred want Sharon to pay for lunch on Saturday?

_____

Vocabulary Building Sentences

> First, underline the word or expression from the vocabulary list in the
> prelistening/reading section. Then write a new sentence, using the same word or
> expression. Follow the model.

MODEL: These old letters aren't <u>worth saving</u>. I'm going to throw them out.

These stamps are worth saving. They might be valuable someday.
_____

1. We gave my teacher a lift to school today.

   _____

2. David's parents will be glad when he gets through school.

   _____

3. I'm sure glad that tomorrow is payday. I'm down to nothing.

   _____

4. Janet's brother was ripped off last week. Someone stole his stereo.

   _____

5. My new boyfriend likes to flirt with other women, so I have to keep an eye on him.

   _____

6. I wish I hadn't ordered so much food; I just got carried away.

   _____

7. We had to toss out the bread because it was old and stale.

   _____

8. I don't like to go to the dentist, but I might as well get it over with.

   _____

9. I have to get used to taking the bus every day.

   _____

10. I don't ever break even when I gamble. I always lose.

    _____

11. I'm going to the store anyway; let me pick up some milk for you.

_____

Word Forms

> Complete the following sentences with the correct word form.

permanent wave   permanent   permanently

1. Last year he moved to Arizona _____

2. She had a _____ and now her hair is very curly.

3. Do you have a _____ address, or are you still staying with friends?

easy   easiest   easier

1. This is the _____ exercise in this lesson.

2. Writing sentences in English is not always _____ for me.

3. It is _____ to lose money than to make it.

Conversation Activities

> Working in groups, discuss the following:

In your native country, who washes the clothes for your family? Is it easier to wash clothes at home than in a laundromat? Some people think that it's more expensive to wash clothes at home than in a laundromat. What do you think? When you were a child, what were you expected to help with at home?

Some people seem to be very lucky. They win prizes and find things others have lost. Have you ever found something valuable? If you have found something, what was it and where were you? If you found a large amount of money, what would you do with it?

Suggested Role-Plays

> Working in groups or in pairs, prepare a dialogue to share with the class. The following topics are suggestions for you to use.

The Laundromat

1. **Participants: Sharon and her sister, Dianne**
   Yesterday, at the laundromat, Sharon threw out an old pair of jeans she thought were hers.

Dianne: Hi. How are things going?

Sharon: Great! The day before yesterday I got my grocery shopping done, yesterday I did all of my laundry, and today I finished all of my studying. I'm looking forward to a fantastic weekend.

Dianne: That's wonderful! I wish I could say the same thing. I've spent most of today organizing my closet. There's just one thing I can't find. My favorite jeans are missing. I know that they are old and worn out, but they're the most comfortable pair of pants I've ever had. Have you seen them?

Finish the dialogue.

2. **Participants: Fred (on the phone) and his parents**
   Fred's older brother has just called his parents to tell them that Fred asked to borrow some money. His parents are worried about him.

Fred's Mom: Hi. I'm glad you're home. I just got a phone call from David, and he said that Fred asked to borrow some money again.

Fred's Dad: I was afraid that might happen. Fred seems to have some trouble managing his money.

Fred's Mom: Maybe he should come back home to live with us.

Fred's Dad: Why don't you give him a call and we can talk about it.

Finish the dialogue.

Listening Comprehension Cloze Passage

> Listen to the tape of the following passage or to your teacher. Fill in the missing words as you hear them.

I have _____ (1) hated machines. I have never bothered to learn to

_____ (2) the oil in my car or change a tire. I had a _____ (3) washing

machine that sat in my house for _____ (4) a year. I always thought it would be

much _____ (5) expensive to repair—even though I had no idea what was wrong

_____ (6) it. I was sure that I _____ (7) afford to get it fixed. For those

_____ (8), I spent months and months dragging all of my laundry through the win-

The Laundromat

ter _____ and the summer heat to the laundromat and paying to wash my
                 9

_____ there instead of having the luxury and _____ of being able
     10   11

to wash my clothes in _____ own home any time I wanted to wash them.
                            12

_____ _____, as I was thanking a friend for changing the
      13   14

_____ in my car, he criticized me for saying that I _____ him be-
       15   16

cause he could _____ things and I couldn't. He got _____ with
                     17   18

me and said that I was able to fix things, but that I just _____ take the time to
                                                                  19

learn how. I _____ about what he said. He was right.
                  20

That very day I went to the library and _____ _____ a book
                                                    21   22

on appliance repair. It took me _____ days to study the section on washing ma-
                                      23

chines. I had to use a dictionary to _____ _____ a lot of unfamiliar
                                           24   25

words. _____ I felt like I knew a little about what I _____ to do, I
            26   27

went to the _____ hardware store to talk about my problem. When I told the
                  28

hardware store clerk what I _____ was wrong with my washing machine, he
                                  29

helped me _____ _____ the parts I needed to repair it. It took me
                30   31

two days of _____, skinned knuckles, and broken fingernails, but I fixed it my-
                  32

self! It didn't cost _____ _____ of money, either.
                          33   34

I know that I will _____ want to repair appliances for a living,
                         35

_____ I do know that I am capable of doing _____ things myself. I
      36   37

just have to be _____ to take the time to learn.
                      38

Final Project

Are you a stuffy person? Often we won't do something or eat something or go some-
place just because it doesn't sound like something we would like.

> Think of something you said you would never do. Think of something you said you
> would never eat or drink. Think of someplace you said you would never go. Choose one
> thing or one place. Who asked you? Where were you when you were asked? What were
> the circumstances? Now, talk about it with your classmates or write about it.

5

The Restaurant

General Warm-Up Questions

How do you feel when you go into a strange place for the first time? Is it different if you are with your friends than with your family? Which is worse? When you are confused, do you think it is better to struggle through by yourself, or have a friend do the talking for you? What do you when you are with a friend who does not speak the language but you do? How does it make you feel when you have to translate for someone?

Some people welcome the challenge of a difficult situation. Other people are more conservative and avoid difficult situations when they can. Do you ever put yourself in a difficult situation on purpose? Do you like to try unusual things?

Prelistening/Reading Study Questions

Why doesn't Sharon like to go to restaurants to eat? What does she usually order when she goes out to eat? What does Fred tell Sharon when she is worried? Do they sit in the smoking or nonsmoking section? When will the waitress come to take their order? Sharon's grandfather had a different use for squid. How did he use them? What does Sharon say she will order for Fred the next time they go out for dinner?

Vocabulary

TO END UP (ordering):   what you finally have or decide to have; what you are left with

TO BAIL SOMEONE OUT: to help someone when he or she is in trouble; often to help financially or emotionally; to give money to release someone for jail

FANCY: decorated; ornate; not plain, not simple

OUT OF MY LEAGUE: something you are not accustomed to; something that often feels too sophisticated, advanced, or difficult

TO MAKE RESERVATIONS: to make arrangements ahead of time; to telephone the place you are going to in advance in order to set a specific time for you to arrive

SPUR OF THE MOMENT: without forethought; a decision to do something that has not been carefully planned or prearranged.

TO HESITATE: to wait before you do or say something

RED SNAPPER: a kind of ocean fish especially popular, as food, on the West Coast

TO BE ALL OUT OF SOMETHING: not to have any more of something

MENU: a written list of food, drinks, and prices in a restaurant

YOU'VE GOT IT!: you understand!

WEIRD: strange, unusual, unexplainable, disturbing

DEEP-FRIED: cooked in a lot of oil or lard, usually in a deep pan

TENTACLES: long, spider-like arms

OCTOPUS: a sea animal which has eight tentacles

'EM: them (This expression is common in fast, casual speech. When you are writing, it should be written as *them*.)

BRAVE: not afraid; strong and courageous

A LA CARTE: listed separately on the menu; not a complete meal

TO STARVE: to be very, very hungry; to be without food

THOUSAND ISLAND DRESSING: salad dressing often made of mayonnaise, tomato sauce, pickles, spices, and chopped hard-cooked eggs

BLUE CHEESE DRESSING: salad dressing often made of cheese, sour cream, mayonnaise, blue cheese, and spices

FRENCH DRESSING: salad dressing usually made with oil, vinegar, and spices

HOUSE DRESSING: a specialty of a particular restaurant, not always the same

TO BE KIDDING: to be pretending, joking, fooling

ESCARGOTS: a French word for small snails usually cooked in a sauce of white wine, butter, garlic, and parsley

TO HAVE COURAGE: to be brave; to have strength

ENCOURAGE: to make someone feel better; to help someone feel he or she can do something

SLIMY: covered with a mucous secretion; slippery

SHELL: a hard or tough outer covering; a framework or exterior cover

THE RESTAURANT

Sharon: I'm glad you suggested going out for dinner, but I'm a little nervous.

Fred: Why are you nervous?

Sharon: Well, to tell you the truth, I usually avoid going to fancy restaurants because I never know what to order. The waiters and waitresses ask so many questions so fast that I almost always end up ordering a hamburger. A hamburger is the one thing I understand.

Fred: Hey, don't be nervous. I'll bail you out if you need help, but I'm sure you'll do OK. The most important thing is to take all the time that you need. Don't let anyone rush you. And don't be afraid to ask questions. It's OK to ask the waiter or waitress to repeat what they've said if you don't understand.

Sharon: OK. If this is all so easy and fun, why do I feel like I'm going to the dentist instead of out to dinner?

Fred: Don't be silly. Come on, you'll have a good time, I promise. Trust me.

(Standing inside the restaurant)

Sharon:	Boy, this sure looks fancy. I've never been to anyplace like this before. What do we do now? Can we just go ahead and sit down somewhere?
Fred:	Nope. We need to wait until someone comes and takes us to a table. The host or hostess will ask how many of us there are, and if we want to sit in the smoking or nonsmoking section.
Sharon:	That's great! I hate to sit next to smokers while I'm eating. Here comes someone who looks like she knows what she's doing.
Hostess:	Good evening. Do you have reservations?
Fred:	No, we don't. It was a spur of the moment decision to go out to eat.
Hostess:	That's OK. We're not too busy right now. It's still pretty early. Are there just the two of you for dinner?
Fred:	Yes, just the two of us.
Hostess:	Smoking or nonsmoking?
Fred:	Nonsmoking, please.
Hostess:	Come right this way. I can give you a nice table over here.

(Seated at a table)

Fred:	Thanks. This is perfect!
Sharon:	Boy, this restaurant sure looks fancy. Are you sure we're in the right place? Remember, I'm used to McDonald's. This is a little out of my league.
Fred:	Shhh. . . . Here comes our waitress.
Waitress:	Good evening. How are you tonight?
Fred:	Just fine, thanks.
Sharon:	Good evening.
Waitress:	My name is Mary. I'll be your waitress for this evening. Can I get you something from the bar first?
Fred:	No, thank you.
Waitress:	OK. Let me tell you about tonight's specials. Our fish is red snapper. It's cooked in a butter and garlic sauce with white wine and mushrooms. We also have pasta primavera. It's fettucine made with fresh vegetables served in a light cream sauce. Here are your menus. I'll give you some time to look at them. The only thing we're all out of is the fresh salmon. I'll be back in a few minutes to take your order.
Fred:	OK. Thank you.

(Reading the menu)

Fred:	What looks good, Sharon?
Sharon:	Boy, there are so many things to choose from. I can't make up my mind. It's a lot easier to order at McDonald's.
Fred:	Take your time. As long as we're still reading the menus, our waitress probably won't come back to the table unless we make eye contact with her to show that we need help. She'll probably wait until we've closed our menus to come and take our order.

The Restaurant

Sharon: OK. Good. That gives me some time. What's quiche?

Fred: Quiche is a pie made with milk and eggs. It sometimes has cheese, vegetables, or bacon in it.

Sharon: That sounds pretty weird to me. What's calamari?

Fred: Calamari is squid. It's usually deep-fried like french fries.

Sharon: You mean the squid that swim around in the ocean and have all those tentacles and look like little octopuses?

Fred: That's right, you've got it!

Sharon: You mean people actually eat them? My grandfather used to use them as bait to catch fish.

Fred: Sure, people eat 'em. You'd be surprised how good they are.

Sharon: No kidding?

Fred: No kidding. They're really great. Trust me.

Sharon: OK. I'm feeling brave. I'll try the calamari.

Fred: Good. I think I'll order the red snapper.

Sharon: Are you going to have the complete dinner, or a la carte?

Fred: I'm starving. I think I'll get the whole dinner. How about you?

Sharon: The whole dinner comes with soup and salad, a drink, and dessert. Hmmm . . . I don't think I'm hungry enough for that much food. I'll just order a la carte. It looks like that still comes with soup or salad.

Fred: OK. Now all we've got to do is close our menus and wait for the waitress to come back.

Sharon: Yeah. Here comes the hard part. This is where she asks all of the fast questions.

Fred: Shhh. . . . Here she comes. I'll help you, remember?

Waitress: Have you decided?

Fred: Sharon?

Sharon: Yes. I'd like the calamari a la carte, please.

Waitress: You have your choice of soup or salad.

Sharon: Ummm . . . salad, please.

Waitress: Tossed green, or spinach?

Sharon: What's the difference?

Waitress: The tossed green is made with lettuce, and the spinach is made with spinach. The spinach salad has chopped hard-boiled eggs and crisp bacon in it, and it's tossed with an oil and vinegar dressing. It's pretty good.

Sharon: OK . . . I think I'll try the spinach salad.

Waitress: Would you like french fries, mashed, or baked potato?

Sharon: French fries, please.

Waitress: What would you like to drink?

Sharon: Do you have tea?

Waitress: Yes, we do. Would you like black or herb tea?

Sharon: I'll have a cup of black tea, please.

The Restaurant

Waitress:	OK. Have you decided, sir?
Fred:	Yes. I'd like the red snapper dinner, please.
Waitress:	You get soup and salad. Would you like tossed green, or spinach?
Fred:	Tossed green.
Waitress:	Thousand Island, blue cheese, French, ranch, or house dressing?
Fred:	What's your house dressing?
Waitress:	It's our specialty. It's an oil and vinegar dressing with herbs.
Fred:	What's the ranch dressing?
Waitress:	The ranch is a creamy garlic dressing.
Fred:	That sounds good. And I'll have a baked potato, please.
Waitress:	Butter, or sour cream and chives?
Fred:	Can I have all three?
Waitress:	Sure. What would you like to drink?
Fred:	I'll just have a glass of water without ice.
Waitress:	OK, fine. I'll be back in a minute with your soup and salads.

(Later, during dinner)

Sharon:	Hey, my food's great! You were right about the calamari. They're delicious!
Fred:	Good. I'm glad you're enjoying them. My red snapper is pretty good, too. Do you want a bite?
Sharon:	Sure, just a taste. Mmmmm . . . the sauce is fantastic! I think I'll order that next time. Here, try the calamari.
Fred:	Are you kidding? They've still got their legs on!
Sharon:	You're the one who told me that they were so good! Don't you like them?
Fred:	I've never had the courage to try them.
Sharon:	Are you kidding? You rat! Next time we go out to dinner, I'm going to order escargots for you.
Fred:	What are escargots?
Sharon:	Snails.
Fred:	You mean those funny little bugs that crawl around the garden? The slimy ones in the shells?
Sharon:	You'd be surprised how good they are. Trust me.
Fred:	OK, you win. I'll taste your calamari.
Sharon:	Now, aren't they good?
Fred:	Hey, you're right. They are good. Can I have another bite? You can have some more of my red snapper.
Sharon:	No way. You'll just have to wait until next time and order them yourself. You know, Fred, I'm really glad I came. It was a lot easier than I thought it would be to order dinner.
Fred:	You did really well, too. It gets easier every time. Trust me.
Sharon:	Now that's encouraging.

The Restaurant

Postlistening/Reading Questions

> Answer in complete sentences.

1. Why doesn't Sharon like to go to restaurants to eat?

   _____

2. What does Sharon usually order when she goes out to eat?

   _____

3. What does Fred tell Sharon when she says she's nervous?

   _____

4. When will the waitress come over to take their order?

   _____

5. How did Sharon's grandfather use squid?

   _____

6. What is the fish special?

   _____

7. What kind of salad dressing does Fred order?

   _____

8. What is quiche?

   _____

9. What does Sharon think about calamari?

   _____

Vocabulary Building Sentences

> First, underline the word or expression from the vocabulary list in the
> prelistening/reading section. Then write a new sentence, using the same word or
> expression. Follow the model.

MODEL: I always end up with my big sister's old clothes. I'd sure like something new once in a while.

I never knew she'd end up marrying a movie star.

_____

1. I thought I'd have to talk to him all night! Thanks for bailing me out.

   _____

2. I'd like to ask that girl out on a date, but she's out of my league.

   _____

3. Janet thinks I'm crazy because I do everything on the spur of the moment.

   _____

4. I wanted to buy strawberries, but the supermarket was all out of them.

   _____

5. All right! He's finally got it! I didn't think he'd ever understand that math problem.

   _____

6. I'm glad breakfast is ready. I'm starved!

   _____

7. You're kidding! You're not really getting married this summer, are you?

   _____

8. The weather has been very weird lately. Yesterday it was very hot, and today it's freezing cold!

   _____

Word Forms

Complete the following sentences with the correct word form.

hesitates   hesitation   hesitant

1. There was too much _____ in his voice. I don't think he really wants to go.

2. I am always _____ when I meet new people.

3. There is a proverb in English that says: "He who _____ is lost."

lie   liar   lying

1. I never know when she is _____ or telling the truth.

2. Do you ever _____ to your parents?

3. He is such a good _____ that no one knows whether to believe him or not.

starve   starvation   starving

1. Some people in the world die of _____ every day.

2. On some diets, you have to _____ yourself.

3. I was _____! That's why I ate all of the potato chips when I got home from school.

brave   bravely   bravery

1. That war hero is well known for his _____ in combat.

2. I am not very _____ when I have to go to the dentist.

3. She fought _____ for her country.

encouragement   encourage   encouraging

1. Fred's teacher said his grades were very _____ this semester.

2. I think it's great that his teacher gave him so much _____

3. My mother always _____ me to study harder.

courage   courageous

1. An astronaut must be very _____ to go into space.

2. How much _____ do you have?

Conversation Activities

Some people feel very comfortable in a fancy restaurant, and others feel uncomfortable. Have you been to a fancy restaurant? If you have, what kind of a restaurant was it? Were you celebrating a special occasion? Would you rather eat in a restaurant or at home? What are the advantages of eating at home?

What strange foods that you have never eaten before would you like to try? What is the most unusual food that you have ever tasted? What is your favorite food? What kind of North American food do you like? In your native country, do people ever share food from the same plate, or does everyone eat from his or her own plate? When a menu is confusing, what do you usually order? Is it difficult for you to ask a waiter or waitress questions about a menu? Where do you like to go out to eat with your family and friends? What is your favorite kind of restaurant?

Suggested Role-Plays

1. **Participants: Mark and Anne (on the phone)**
   Mark and Anne met a week ago at a party. Mark has been trying to get up enough courage to ask Anne out on a date. He has just called her on the phone.

   Mark: Hello? Is this Anne?
   Anne: Yes. Who is this?
   Mark: It's Mark. We met at the party last week.
   Anne: What party? I went to more than one.
   Mark: The one at John's house. Don't you remember me? I'm the one who likes jazz music and dancing salsa.
   Anne: Oh, yeah. Now I remember. You're a pretty good dancer. Sure, now I remember you. What's up?

   Finish the dialogue.

2. **Participants: Anne, Mark, Janet, John, and Dennis, the waiter**
   The two couples are at an elegant restaurant. They have ordered dinner and are waiting for their meals to arrive. They have waited a long time and are ready to ask if there is something wrong, when they overhear loud, angry voices coming from the kitchen.

   John: I really like this restaurant. I've been here several times before. The food's always good.

   Janet: Does it always take this time to get served? I'm starved.

   John: I don't understand what's taking so long. Dennis is a really good waiter. This is pretty weird.

   Anne: Maybe you should say something, John. You're the one who's been here before.

   Kitchen voices: I'm not going to take this anymore! [CRASH! BANG!]

   Finish the dialogue.

3. **Participants: Nancy and Janet (and two or three people at the next table)**
   Nancy and Janet, who both hate cigarette smoke, have ordered their food and have just been served when some noisy people sit down at the next table and light up cigarettes.

   Janet: Hmmm . . . this looks great! Just look at this wonderful steak. We had to wait a long time, but it was worth waiting for, wasn't it?

   Nancy: It sure was. We've got a great table, too. Right by the window where we can watch everyone.

   Janet: Yup. It just couldn't be more perfect.

   (The people at the other table sit down.)

   Finish the dialogue.

Listening Comprehension Cloze Passage

> Listen to the tape of the following passage or to your teacher. Fill in the missing words as you hear them.

1. As it _____ more expensive to eat in restaurants, people are becoming
        1

_____ willing to accept food or situations they are not happy with. If you are
   2

_____ a restaurant and served something that is not of good
   3

_____, or you are seated at a _____ table close to the kitchen,
   4   5

what do you do?

What we _____ to do depends on several things. First, it
_____ on where we are. Some restaurants seem more intimidating than others.
If the _____ or waitress seems very busy or _____, it is more difficult to _____ food back or ask to be seated at another table. You
_____ have to get the attention of _____ busy or unfriendly waiter
or waitress. Secondly, if the problem is with the food, it _____
_____ what the problem is. If the food is not spoiled, but _____
not hot enough, some of us will eat it _____ rather than send it back. Sometimes we're just too _____ to wait for another order. The third
_____ is who we are with at the restaurant. If we are with
someone we want to _____, we may be too embarrassed to send something
back or ask for a _____ table. If you are with your girlfriend's
_____ whom you just met, do you send something back _____ if
it is terrible? Another _____ to consider if we send something back is that often
we will have to wait _____ our new order comes while everyone else at the table eats, and _____ we will have to eat later when everyone else
_____ finished.

Whatever we do when we are in a _____ situation, it is
_____ that we not be afraid to _____ _____
_____ what we believe is right. When we are paying to eat in a restaurant, we are
_____ for good _____ and good food. Sometimes it is impor-
tant to be _____. It is possible to ask for something graciously and kindly with–
out embarrassing ourselves or the people _____ us. The advantages of
_____ _____ and asking for better food and service are obvious.
We _____ better food and service!

2.   One of my _____ restaurant stories happened when I was a junior in high
1

school. I went to _____ city to have dinner at a very _____ restau-
2   3

rant. There were four of us. I was with my _____, who went to the local col-
4

lege, and my _____ friend was with her date, who was _____ a
5   6

college student. It was the first time we had gone to the _____ for dinner to-
7

gether, and the first time I had _____ _____ _____
8   9   10

my date. We were all trying very hard to impress _____ other with our ele-
11

gance, sophistication, and good manners.

_____ our dates had made reservations well in advance at the popular
12

restaurant, we had a _____ table right in the middle where we could watch ev-
13

eryone and be seen by everyone else. Halfway _____ our elegant dinner, my
14

friend and I _____ ourselves to go to the ladies' room. Our dates, using their
15

best manners, _____ _____ when we did. There was one major
16   17

problem: Earlier, _____ we were all seated at the table, my date realized that
18

_____ pants had come unzipped. What he _____ know was that
19   20

when he zipped his _____ back up, he accidentally caught the tablecloth in his
21

zipper, _____ when he stood up, the tablecloth moved _____
22   23

him. He sat right back down and tried to get the tablecloth unstuck, but _____
24

unsuccessful. By this time everyone in the restaurant was _____ us. My friend
25

and I just stood there—_____ didn't know what to do. Two of the waiters
26

came _____ to our table and removed all of the plates, _____, and
27   28

silverware from the _____. My very embarrassed date got up and walked into
29

the men's _____ holding the rolled up _____ in front of him.
30   31

Twenty minutes later, he came _____ to the table. He said that the waiters had
32

to get _____ scissors and cut the tablecloth free.
33

Final Project

1. Think about an interesting experience you had when you were in a restaurant. Discuss your experience with classmates, role-play the experience with and for your classmates, or write a composition about it.

2. Go to three different restaurants and compare prices for a cup of coffee, a dinner salad, two main dishes, and a dessert. Report on your findings to the class.

3. Go into a restaurant and ask the owner or manager to give you one of the menus. (Most will give you a copy without hesitation.) Bring the menu to class and tell the other students what you would order if you had all the money you needed to order anything you wanted. What would you eat, and how much would it cost? How much would you pay for tax and for a tip? If you didn't get good service, would you leave the same amount of money for a tip?

4. Look at the same menu. Choose a combination of foods that would provide the best nutritional balance. Could you ask for substitutions or changes in the way things are cooked to make the food more nourishing and healthy?

6

The Traffic Ticket

General Warm-Up Questions

Read the following questions before you begin. They will help you to focus on the topic covered in this chapter.

Some people are very good at understanding and fixing mechanical things. Are you? What can you fix? Who generally takes care of things in your house when they need to be repaired? Is it important for everyone to know how to do simple repairs?

If you are driving in your car, and you hear a strange noise coming from your engine, what do you do? Have you ever been in a difficult or unusual situation where you had to solve a problem by yourself? What was it, and where were you?

Prelistening/Reading Study Questions

Read the following questions before you listen to or read the dialogue. Take a few moments to think about them. They will help you understand the dialogue when you begin.

Where is all of the traffic coming from? How fast is the Trans Am going? When they see a police car behind them, what does Sharon tell Fred to do? What are the three things the policeman asks Fred for? What is wrong with Fred's car? How much time does he have to fix things that are wrong with his car? Where does he have to mail the ticket? Where are Fred and Sharon going next?

Vocabulary

YEAH: yes (This expression is common in fast, casual speech. When you are writing, it should always be written as *yes*.)

TO TURN INTO: to become or change

WHOA: wait a minute (This expression is common only in casual speech.)

TO CUT IN FRONT OF: to move or to push your way in front of someone or something

TRANS AM: An American-made fast car

CHEVY: Chevrolet—a popular make of American car

CUTE: attractive, nice looking

TO CHECK (SOMETHING OR SOMEONE) OUT: to look at, to study, to evaluate

TAKE IT EASY: relax; don't worry; be happy

HOT ON THE TRAIL OF: close to catching someone or something

GLOVE COMPARTMENT: a small storage cabinet in the dashboard of an automobile

A CITATION: a ticket; a piece of paper issued by a police officer that states what is wrong

VIOLATIONS: things or actions that are wrong or illegal; breaking rules

HEADLIGHT: a clear light mounted on each side of the front of vehicle

TAIL LIGHT: a red warning light mounted on each side of the back of a vehicle

DRIVING RECORD: the information stored in a computer at the Department of Motor Vehicles that says if you have been in accidents, have moving violations or parking tickets

A FINE: money paid as a penalty for doing something wrong or against the law

TO SIGN OFF: to approve something with an official signature; to say goodnight or goodbye

JUST ISN'T YOUR NIGHT (DAY): this is a bad time for you; you are not lucky right now

TO PUT SOMETHING MILDLY: to understate something; to make something sound less serious than it is

CRAZIES: crazy people; people who act strangely

NOTHING TO SNEEZE AT: something that is important; something that has more significance than it is given

I'D: I would (This expression is common in fast, casual speech.)

IN ONE PIECE: not damaged or harmed; safe and well

TO TAKE A RISK: to take a chance; to do something that may not be completely safe

TO PART WITH (SOMETHING OR SOMEONE): to give something up; to relinquish something; to let someone go

'EM: them (This pronunciation is common in fast, casual speech. When you are writing, it should be written as *them*.)

THE TRAFFIC TICKET

Fred: Boy, you can sure tell it's Friday night. Look at all the traffic. It's all those people coming from the valley.

Sharon: Yeah, just what we need. I can't believe it. Our nice little town is turning into a big city.

Fred: Whoa! Wait a minute! Did you see that guy in the Trans Am cut right in front of me? He must be going 80 at least!

Sharon: Yeah. Where are all the cops when you need them?

Fred: Hey, check out that redhead in the Chevy. She's pretty cute! Oh-oh. There's a Highway Patrolman coming up behind me, and he's got his red light on. What did I do wrong?

Sharon: Relax. Take it easy. He can't be after you. You're not speeding, or anything. He's probably hot on the trail of that Trans Am. Just slow down and pull over into the right-hand lane. He'll just go around you.

Fred: OK, OK. Hey, why is he staying behind me? He's not passing. He's slowing down. Damn, I'm sure that I wasn't doing anything wrong.

(Stopped at the side of the road)

Officer: Good evening.

Fred: Good evening, officer.

The Traffic Ticket

Officer:	May I see your driver's license, vehicle registration, and proof of insurance, please?
Fred:	Here's my license . . . .
Officer:	Would you take it out of your wallet, please?
Fred:	Yes, sir. Here it is. I haven't cleaned the glove compartment in a while . . . I don't see the registration anywhere. Oh, here it is. Here's my insurance card, too.
Officer:	Would you mind stepping out of the car, please?
Fred:	No, certainly officer. But I don't understand what the problem is. I'm sure I wasn't speeding.
Officer:	Your driving is just fine. The problem is with your car. You've got a headlight out and a taillight out, too.
Fred:	There's a headlight out?
Officer:	Come on around the front of the car and take a look. Do you see anything?
Fred:	No . . . .
Officer:	Then it's out. I'm going to have to write you a citation.
Fred:	Oh, no. I'll get the lights fixed right away, I promise. Do you have to give me a ticket? I wasn't doing anything wrong.
Officer:	Driving at night with a headlight and a taillight out is doing something wrong. You could have caused an accident.
Fred:	Yes, sir.
Officer:	Let me explain this ticket to you. You will have 15 days to repair the headlight and the taillight. Within 15 days, go to any Highway Patrol office, and have a police officer check out your car to make sure that the lights are both working again. Then, after the officer has signed off the ticket, mail it to the municipal court. For now, I want you to get off the freeway and to avoid night driving until your lights are repaired.
Fred:	OK. Excuse me, sir. Is this ticket going to cost me money? Will it go on my driving record? I've got a pretty good record.
Officer:	The ticket itself won't cost you any money, but you'll have to pay to fix the lights. There's no fine, and this violation will not go on your driving record. Will you sign this ticket, please?
Fred:	OK.
Officer:	Have a nice evening, now.
Fred:	Thank you, sir. You, too.

(Driving away)

Sharon:	I guess this just isn't your night, is it?
Fred:	That's putting it mildly. I can't believe my luck. With all the crazies on the road, I get stopped because I have a few lights out.
Sharon:	Hey, a few lights is serious business. It's nothing to sneeze at. I'm riding around with you, remember? I'd like to get home in one piece.
Fred:	Yeah, you're right. I knew the lights were out. I shouldn't have taken the risk. I just didn't want to part with the money to get 'em fixed.
Sharon:	Well, now you've got no choice. What'd he say—15 days?
Fred:	Yup. Fifteen days, but I'll get it done sooner than that. I should get some money from my brother on Monday. In the meantime, I've got an idea.
Sharon:	What's that?
Fred:	You know that trip we were going to take to the museum?

The Traffic Ticket

Sharon: Sure, I remember.

   Fred: How about if we take the bus and forget about driving for a few days?

Sharon: That sounds like a great idea.

Postlistening/Reading Questions

Answer in complete sentences.

1. Where is all of the traffic coming from?

_____

2. How fast was the Trans Am going?

_____

3. What does Sharon tell Fred to do when he sees the police car behind them?

_____

4. What two things does the policeman ask Fred for?

_____

5. What is wrong with his car?

_____

6. How much time does Fred have to fix his car?

_____

7. Where does he have to mail the ticket?

_____

8. What do you think will happen if Fred doesn't mail in the ticket on time?

_____

9. How much does Fred have to pay for the ticket?

_____

10. Why does Sharon think it's important to get the lights fixed?

_____

11. Where are they going next?

_____

Vocabulary Building Sentences

First, underline the word or expression from the vocabulary list in the prelistening/reading section. Then write a new sentence, using the same word or expression. Follow the model.

MODEL: I wanted to buy a new jacket, but I didn't want <u>to part with</u> the money.

I don't think Anne's baby will ever part with his favorite blanket.

1. My boyfriend turns into the wolfman when the moon is full.

   _____

2. She always tries to cut in front of me in the cafeteria line.

   _____

3. The police were hot on the trail of the killers.

   _____

4. Take it easy! I'm sure we'll get there on time.

   _____

5. I'm going to sign off for now. I have to get back to my studying.

   _____

6. It just isn't my night. I had a fight with David, too.

   _____

7. You're getting a divorce, and you just say you've got a little problem? That's putting it mildly.

   _____

8. I wish you'd drive more carefully. I want to get home in one piece.

   _____

9. My brother took a risk when he decided to move out on his own.

   _____

Word Forms

Complete the following sentences with the correct word form.

violate   violation   violating

1. It is a _____ to walk across the street when the light is red.

2. Don't _____ the no-smoking ordinance.

3. _____ the law can be very expensive.

Conversation Activities

Working in groups, discuss the following:

Did you ever have an experience with the police? If you did, what happened? In the United States, everyone has rights. What are your rights if you are stopped by the police or if a police officer comes to your house? Is it important to know what your rights are? If you don't know the answer to this question, where do you think you would be able to find out? Where does the American English expression "cop" or "copper" come from? Where could you find out if you don't know? Are the police the same in every country? Do you think that all police officers are honest and fair? Fred was stopped because he had a headlight out. Is that as bad as driving too fast?

Suggested Role-Plays

Working in groups or in pairs, prepare a dialogue to share with the class. The following topics are suggestions for you to use.

1. **Participants: Fred and the auto supply saleswoman**
   Fred has decided to try to replace the headlight and taillight on his car himself. He doesn't know anything about cars, so he will need some help.

   Fred: I have to buy a headlight and a taillight for my car.
   Saleswoman: What kind of a car do you have?
   Fred: It's an old green Ford.
   Saleswoman: I need a little more information than that. It sounds like you don't know a lot about fixing cars.

   Finish the dialogue.

2. **Participants: Policeman John Adams and his wife Joan**
   John Adams comes home after a hard day at work. He has forgotten that he promised his wife they would go to a dinner party with some people from their childrens' school.

John: Hi. Is anybody home?

Joan: I'm out here in the kitchen.

John: Oh, hi honey. How was your day?

Joan: It's been crazy around here. I finished all of the laundry, entered our expense and income data into the computer, got the shopping done, and took the kids to the doctor for their checkups. When the baby-sitter canceled, it took me two hours on the phone to find another one. She'll be here in less than an hour. You're a little late tonight, aren't you?

John: I had a terrible day. I had to deal with three accidents, and I gave out about a dozen tickets. The easiest was to a guy whose lights didn't work, and the toughest was a high-speed chase with a guy in a Trans Am who was going about 90 miles an hour on a mountain road. All afternoon I've been thinking about coming home, taking a hot shower, and stretching out in front of the TV all night. It sure feels good to come home and relax. What's for dinner? Did you say something about a babysitter?

Finish the dialogue.

The Traffic Ticket

Listening Comprehension Cloze Passage

> Listen to the tape of the following passage or to your teacher. Fill in the missing words as you hear them.

There are _____ people in the United States who believe that there are cer-
1

tain jobs that _____ be done by women, and _____ jobs that
2   3

should be done by men. What do you _____?
4

For many years, women have been _____ to stay at home and take care of
5

their husbands and _____. In the 1950s, when women went to college, they
6

went to _____ their MRS degree—that is, they went to find husbands. They
7

were encouraged by their _____ and by much of society to marry doctors and
8

lawyers —_____ to become doctors or lawyers. Women often
9

_____ home economics, nursing, or teaching. They studied things that would
10

make them _____ marketable to prospective husbands. _____
11   12

_____ _____, they studied things that would make them better
13   14

wives, cooks, housekeepers, and caregivers to the children they would have.

In the 1950s, men were _____ that it wasn't masculine to do work that was
15

traditionally done by women. While women learned to be good housewives and mothers,

_____ were studying to be able to _____ in the job
16   17

_____ with other men. Women studied home economics, while men
18

_____ to become chefs or restaurant owners; women studied to become
19

_____, while men learned to become doctors; women studied to
20

_____ teachers, while men learned to become professors.
21

Things have changed since the 1950s for many _____. Two very significant
22

factors were the free speech _____ of the 1960s and the Vietnam War. Now, it is
23

not _____ to see women holding jobs that were _____ held by
24   25

men. There are _____ police officers, plumbers, carpenters, doctors, engineers,
26

bus _____, pilots, telephone repair workers, and soldiers, just to name a few.
27

Just _____ society is beginning to accept women in jobs traditionally held by
28

men, it is more _____ for men to do jobs traditionally held by women. There
29

are men who _____ to stay home and take care of the house and children; there
30

are _____ nurses and male flight attendants. It will take a long
31

_____ for all of us to adjust to all of _____ changes, but it will
32   33

happen.

Final Project

Do you think women should work in dangerous jobs like police work or the military?
Prepare a persuasive speech to give to your class about why you think this should or
should not be.

7

The Bus Stop

General Warm-Up Questions

Read the following questions before you begin. They will help you to focus on the topic covered in this chapter.

When people travel, they like to do many different kinds of things. Some like to ride around on public transportation to see the sights, some like to shop and go to restaurants where they can sit and watch people, and others like to go to galleries, concerts, and museums. Have you been to a museum? If so, where and when? What did you see? Have you been to a concert? If so, where was the concert and what kind of music did you hear? If you could spend a day at the beach or in a museum, which would you do and why? Did you ever go on a field trip with your classmates? If so, where did you go and when? Did you go by bus?

Prelistening/Reading Study Questions

Read the following questions before you listen to or read the dialogue. Take a few moments to think about them. They will help you understand the dialogue when you begin.

Where does Sharon want to go? Why doesn't Fred want to take a taxi? What is the name of the street where Fred and Sharon are going? Who do they ask for help? How else could they have gotten help? When do they have to transfer? Do you think that they are in a strange city? If you think they are in a strange city, why do you think so? Why don't they go to the museum?

Vocabulary

TO TAKE IN: to go see; to look at

TO FORK OUT BIG BUCKS: to spend a lot of money

MA'AM: a contraction of *madam*; commonly used as a polite manner of address to a woman who is older than you are (Note: *Ma'am* is a more common manner of address in Southern dialects than in Northern dialects of American English.)

GRUMPY: to be unhappy or unpleasant

YELLOW PAGES: the part of the telephone book which has advertisements for businesses and services

TO TRANSFER: to send from one place to another

COULD'VE: could have (This is common in fast, casual speech.)

TAKE IT EASY: relax; calm down; don't worry

TRAFFIC: movement of cars, buses, trucks, ships, planes, or other vehicles in or through a certain area

TO CONNECT WITH: to meet; to contact; to get together with

The Bus Stop

NOT TO WORRY: don't worry

TO KICK BACK: to relax; to take it easy

A SEC: a second; a very short period of time (This pronunciation is common in fast, casual speech. When you are writing, it should always be written as *a second*.)

D'YA: do you (This is common in fast, casual speech. When you are writing, these words should always be written as *do you*.)

GOTTA: (have) got to (This expression is common in fast, casual speech. When you are writing, it should be written as *got to*.)

TO MAKE IT: to be on time; to get something done or go somewhere when you want (in time)

WE'VE: we have (This is common in fast, casual speech.)

TO LIVE AND LEARN: to learn more as you get older

TO BE ON THE SAFE SIDE: to be careful; to protect yourself

THERE'RE: there are (This expression is common in fast, casual speech. When you are writing, it should be written as *there are*.)

REMODELING: fixing something up; changing something to make it better, newer, more convenient

BUS STOP

Sharon: Hey, this is a great place, huh?

Fred: Yeah, I guess so. But remember, this was your idea, not mine. I guess I'm ready to take in the art museum.

Sharon: Great. Let's take a cab.

Fred: Come on, that's too expensive. I'm not going to fork out big bucks for a cab. We'll take a city bus.

Sharon: But we don't know how the buses run here.

Fred: Well, it should be easy enough to find out.

Sharon: We could ask that bus driver over there, I guess.

Fred: Not that one. He's a Greyhound driver. We need a city bus driver. Here's one. Excuse me, ma'am. Could you tell us how to get to Pacific and Fifth?

Driver: You take the 55 and transfer to the 103 at Pacific. The 55 runs every 15 minutes, and the 103 runs on the half-hour. You can get a schedule on the rack over there.

Fred: Thank you, ma'am.

Driver: Don't mention it.

Sharon: She seemed a little grumpy.

Fred: You'd be grumpy too if people asked you the same questions day after day. We could have called the bus company and gotten the information we needed.

Sharon: Yeah, but we didn't know the name of the company.

Fred: We probably could've looked in the yellow pages under "Bus Lines."

Sharon: Well, live and learn. Hey! Here comes bus number 55. It's right on time, too!

(Boarding the bus)

Driver: I can't take your dollar bill. We only take exact change.

Sharon: Oh, nuts! I don't have any change.

Fred: Wait a sec. I know I've got it here somewhere.

Sharon: Great! Say, driver, could you tell us when we get to Pacific Avenue? We've gotta change to another bus.

Driver: Then you're each going to need a transfer.

Fred: Oh, that's right. Thanks.

Sharon: Boy! Look at all the traffic. We'll be lucky if we can connect with the 103.

Fred: Not to worry. Just kick back and enjoy the ride. It's sure nice not to be driving for a change.

Sharon: But this is taking so much longer than I thought it would. I sure hope we make it on time.

Fred: Take it easy, we'll make it.

Driver: Jefferson Street. Next stop, Pacific Avenue.

Fred: Oh. That's us. Ours is the next stop.

Sharon: Thank you, driver.

(Getting off the bus)

Fred: Well, it looks like we've missed the 103.

Sharon: How d'ya know?

Fred: I just saw it go by.

Sharon: Sometimes a driver can hold another bus by calling ahead on his telephone, if he knows someone needs it.

Fred: Buses have telephones?

Sharon: Yeah. Most of them do. That way if there's an emergency, they can get help quickly.

Fred: We're a little too late for that. We should have thought to ask him to call ahead before we got off.

Sharon: It could be worse. We could be on our way to school or to work instead of the art museum.

Fred: That's true, but if I were going to school or to work, I'd be in my car and I'd leave my house early just to be on the safe side. I hate being late, especially to class.

Sharon: I guess during the week there're probably more buses running.

The Bus Stop

Fred: There sure are. They're all listed here in the schedule. Hey, wait a minute. There's a bus that goes to Pacific and Fifth every 45 minutes from the next corner. See? It's right here in the schedule!

Sharon: Fantastic! Let's hurry so we don't miss that one, too.

(One hour later)

Fred: Finally! There's the museum. Do you see it? It's right across the street.

Sharon: All right! We made it! Say, what's that sign out in front?

Fred: It looks like . . . oh, no. I can't believe it. The sign says:"Museum Closed for Remodeling."

Postlistening/Reading Questions

Answer in complete sentences.

1. Where does Sharon want to go?

_____

2. Why doesn't Fred want to take a cab?

_____

3. What street are Fred and Sharon going to?

_____

The Bus Stop

4. Whom do they ask for help?

_____

5. How else could they have gotten help?

_____

6. When do they have to transfer?

_____

7. Do you think they are in a strange city? Why?

_____

8. Why don't they go to the museum?

_____

Vocabulary Building Sentences

First, underline the word or expression from the vocabulary list in the prelistening/reading section. Then write a new sentence, using the same word or expression. Follow the model.

MODEL: I'd like to stay home today and just <u>kick back</u>.

We just kicked back all weekend. _____

1. I want to take in that movie at the Del Mar.

_____

2. Did you have to fork out big bucks for that car?

_____

3. I'll connect with you in the library at 10.

_____

4. If I finish my homework, I'll try to make it to the party.

_____

5. I didn't know you had been married four times! Well, you live and learn.

_____

6. I like to be on the safe side, so I go to the dentist for a checkup once a year.

_____

Word Forms

grumpier   grumpy   grump

1. My little brother is a _____.

2. He is _____ than I am.

3. Even when I make him laugh, he's still _____.

transferable   transferring   transfer

1. Do you plan to _____ to UCSC?

2. I hope all of my classes are _____.

3. My friend is _____ to San Jose State in the fall.

Conversation Activities

Some people think bus drivers have a hard job. Do you agree? Are most bus drivers nice to their passengers? What is it like to travel in a strange city? Have you ever gotten lost? If you have, how did it make you feel? Should people ride buses instead of drive cars?

Sometimes when we don't want to do something and someone talks us into doing it, we have more fun than we thought we would have. Has this ever happened to you? Have you been to an art gallery or museum? Where was it, and what did you see? Was it your idea to go, or was it someone else's idea? Did you ever plan to go somewhere special and find out that the place was closed? If so, where was it and when?

Suggested Role-Plays

1. **Participants: Janet and David**
   David has invited Janet to an art museum to see a new modern art exhibit he likes very

much. Janet wants to be with David, but she's too embarrassed to tell him that she doesn't understand modern art.

David: I'm glad that you could come with me today, Janet.

Janet: I am, too. I have been looking forward to spending the day together.

David: You're going to love this exhibit. Ah, here we are. Look at this wonderful Escher. The optical illusions he has created are truly remarkable. Just look at this woodblock. The birds flying above the waves become fish swimming beneath. He did this in 1938. What do you think of it?

Finish the dialogue.

2. **Participants: Sharon and John, David and Janet**
David and Janet have just ordered lunch in a restaurant. Janet is trying to forget John, her old boyfriend, when he walks into the restaurant with another woman, holding hands and laughing.

David: This restaurant was a great idea, Janet. I've never had Ethiopian food, and I've wanted to try it for a long time.

Janet: I used to come here a lot with my old boyfriend. But that's all over with. The food is great. You don't mind eating with your hands, do you?

David: Not at all. I'm always ready to try something new. Boy. Look at that couple who just came in the door. They sure look like they're having a great time. Hey, Janet. Don't you know that guy?

Finish the dialogue.

Listening Comprehension Cloze Passage

> Listen to the tape of the following passage or to your teacher. Fill in the missing words as you hear them.

If you need to walk _____ in the evening, there are some very important

1

_____ to consider. You should really _____ go out alone late at

2   3

night. If you plan to go to the library, for instance, _____ to a friend's

4

_____, ask a friend to go with you. It's always nice to have _____,

5   6

and you won't have to walk home by yourself. This idea of two people _____,

7

hiking, swimming, or doing anything together in an area that may not be entirely

_____ is often called the "buddy system." _____ in

8   9

_____ is another word for *friend*, and friends take care of each other.
10

That's the _____ idea of the buddy stystem. You walk together to
11

_____ each other company and to _____ _____
12   13   14

_____ each other.
15

When you are walking, it's important to walk briskly _____ confidently.
16

You want to appear to be in _____ control, and you _____ want to
17   18

appear vulnerable and frightened. If someone _____ to stop you or ask for
19

money, continue walking. Don't _____ a conversation with someone you don't
20

know unless you're in a very safe place _____ there are other people around.
21

It's always a good _____ to take a self-defense class. They are usually
22

_____ through all college programs, adult schools, and local community pro-
23

grams. Self-defense _____ are designed to teach common _____.
24   25

It is much better not to let yourself get into an uncomfortable situation _____ to
26

have to worry about getting out of a _____ situation.
27

_____, if you know that you're going to be late, the _____
28   29

thing that you can do is to make _____ for your transportation home before you
30

go out for the evening. If you have done that in _____, you will be able to relax
31

and not worry _____ how to get home.
32

Final Project

1. Tell your classmates about a scary experience you had. Were you alone?
2. Tell them about an experience you had in a strange city or town. Did someone help you?
3. Get a city bus map. Find a museum, cultural center, or park on the map. Write down clear directions you could give someone to tell them how to get there from your school or home.
4. Tell one of your classmates how to get to a bus station, airport, or shopping center. After you have given directions, ask your classmate to give directions to the same place to someone else. Listen carefully. Are the directions the same as the ones you gave? If there were any changes, discuss the changes and why you think they happened.

8

A Place to Rent

General Warm-Up Questions

Read the following questions before you begin. They will help you to focus on the topic covered in this chapter.

Many young people in the United States live by themselves or with their friends before they get married. Do you think it's better to live at home with your family than by yourself? Could you convince your parents that you should be able to live in an apartment with a friend? Would your family be upset if you shared an apartment with someone of the opposite sex? What kinds of things can you do when you are living alone that you can't do when you're living with your parents? Are there things that you can do when you're living with your parents that you couldn't do if you were living alone or with friends?

Prelistening/Reading Study Questions

Read the following questions before you listen to or read the dialogue. Take a few moments to think about them. They will help you understand the dialogue when you begin.

Why does Fred want to move? Where does Sharon tell him to look for rentals? Why does Sharon want to go to the campus housing office? What does the housing office secretary give Fred? Do you think some people would rather have female roommates? If so, why? If you looked in the newspaper, where would you find the rental information? Are there places on campus where Fred can find out about rooms for rent?

Vocabulary

OFFHAND: something that comes into your mind casually; without careful thought or consideration

YUP: yes (This expression is common in fast, casual speech. In writing, it should be *yes*.)

ROWDY: noisy and often uncontrolled; not reserved

'EM: them (This is common in fast, casual speech. When you are writing, it should be written as *them*.)

THEY'D: they would (This is common in fast, casual speech. When you are writing, it should be written as *they would*.)

THERE'RE: there are (This expression is common in fast, casual speech. When you are writing, it should be written as *there are*.)

BULLETIN BOARD: a special place or section on a wall where people are allowed to post notices advertising items for sale, services, housing, and so on.

YEAH: yes (This is common in fast, casual speech. When you are writing, it should always be written as *yes*.)

YA': you (Note that the pronunciation is the same as it is for *yeah*. This is common in fast, casual speech. When you are writing, it should always be written as *you*.)

WHERE'S: where is (This is common in fast, casual speech. When you are writing, it should be written as *where is*.)

TO FEEL FUNNY: to feel strange; to feel awkward

SENSIBLE: showing clear thinking; practical; of good judgment

TO BE ALL SET: to be ready to do something; to be prepared for something

POSITIVELY: deninitely; without a doubt

HERE WE GO AGAIN: when you recognize that you are saying or doing the same thing that you have said or done at an earlier time

IT'S THE SAME OLD STORY: when you recognize that you are hearing the same thing that you have heard at an earlier time

WEIRD: strange, unusual, unexplainable, disturbing

TO JUMP RIGHT OUT AT: to be very noticeable; to be obvious

NO KIDDING: really? is that true?

TO BE ABLE TO HANDLE (SOMETHING OR SOMEONE): to be able to tolerate or to deal with someone or something

NOT TO BE ABLE TO HANDLE (SOMETHING OR SOMEONE): to be unable to tolerate or deal with something or someone

A TOTAL SLOB: someone who is not careful about his or her appearance; someone who is not clean

STEREOTYPE: seeing all people of a particular sex, race, or religion as the same

TO BE OFF (SOMEONE'S) LIST: to give up on something or someone; to decide something or someone is not worth the trouble to deal with

TO BE WORTH A SHOT: to be worth a try; to have enough value to warrant an effort

A PAIN: something you do not like to do; a person or thing that is boring, troublesome

TO DISCRIMINATE: to prefer one group of people more than another group of people

TO GO RIGHT AWAY: to sell or rent quickly

UTILITIES: services like electricity, heat, and water often provided by public companies

TO TAKE DOWN: to write, to note something

TO CHECK (SOMETHING OR SOMEONE) OUT: to look at, to study, to evaluate

WANT ADS: newspaper advertisements saying something or someone is wanted

 # A PLACE TO RENT

Fred: Hey, Sharon, you're just the person I'm looking for. Do you know anyone who's looking for a roommate?

Sharon: Not offhand. Why? Are you thinking of moving?

Fred: Yup. Actually, I've been thinking about it for a long time. The family I'm staying with is really nice, but they're really quiet. You know my own family's pretty rowdy, and I'm used to more noise. The family I'm staying with doesn't talk to me that much, and I feel funny bringing my friends home and playing my music.

Sharon: Have you talked to them about it?

Fred: Yeah. A little. I told 'em that I thought I wanted to find a place to live with students my own age. They said they'd be sorry to see me go, but that they understood completely.

Sharon: That's good. There're several places you can look for rentals. You can look in the newspaper. You can also check with friends. If ya' look on the bulletin boards here on campus you might find something, and you can also check at the student housing office. John found an apartment through them last month.

Fred: Where's the student housing office?

Sharon: It's across campus by that big new building.

Fred: Oh, yeah! I never knew what that office was for. Do ya' wanna come with me?

Sharon: Sure. Anything's better than studying.

(A few minutes later)

Sharon: Here we are. It's right through these big double doors.

(Inside the office)

Fred: Excuse me, do you have a list of rentals for students?

Secretary: Yes, we do. Are you looking for a room in a house or an apartment?

Fred: A room in a house would be fine. I don't think I want to live all by myself.

Secretary: OK. Here is a binder with the listings of rooms for rent. Please don't take it out of the office, and bring it right back when you're finished with it. You can sit right on one of those chairs.

Fred: OK. thanks.

Secretary: Sure, happy to help.

Sharon: We can sit down over here, Fred. Do you have a piece of paper and a pencil so you can take down some phone numbers and addresses?

Fred: Now, that sounds like a brilliant idea. OK, I'm all set. Let's start looking. I'm going to think good thoughts. I know if I think positively, I'll find just the right thing. It should jump right out of the page at me, right?

Sharon: Will you get serious and start looking?

Fred: Hmmmm . . . wanted: female roommate, nonsmoking vegetarian. That rules me out.

Sharon: At least you're a nonsmoking vegetarian.

Fred: Yeah, but I'm the wrong sex. Here's another one. Oh-oh. Here we go again. It's the same old story. They want a woman roommate, too. Look. Another one. Why does everyone want female roommates?

Sharon: It does seem weird, doesn't it? I think that some people think that women are cleaner and quieter than men.

Fred: No kidding? Do you believe that?

Sharon: Not really. I know some very neat men and some women who are total slobs. I don't think you can stereotype people like that.

A Place to Rent

Fred: Well, I sure wish the people who were looking for roommates felt the same way you do. Look, here's another one. Female roommate wanted. This is the pits. Isn't there some sort of law against discrimination in housing?

Sharon: Yeah, there is, but it doesn't include sharing houses or apartments with other people.

Fred: That doesn't seem very fair. Hey! Wait just a minute here! Here's one. This is too good to be true! Listen to this, Sharon:Roommate wanted:male vegetarian to share house with three college students. Close to campus, low rent, plus share of utilities. Sounds perfect! Looking for someone who doesn't mind being around smokers. Oh-oh. I didn't read far enough. I couldn't handle sharing a house with smokers. Too bad. Until I got to the smoking part, it looked great.

Sharon: Yup. That one would be off my list, too. See any more?

Fred: Here's one. Everything sounds good except the price. It's too expensive. Here's another one that doesn't sound bad, but it's a little farther from school than I wanted. Hmmmm . . . .

Sharon: There are only a few more pages. After we finish here, you might want to go grab a copy of the newspaper and look in the want ad section. The problem is that most of the good places go right away. It's a good idea to go down to the newspaper office and pick up a copy as soon as it comes out. You might want to put up an ad on a few bulletin boards yourself.

Fred: What bulletin boards?

Sharon: They're all over the place. There is a big one right here outside the student housing office, above the stairs. They're all over town, too, in stores and in laundromats.

Fred: I guess it's worth a shot. Well, I might as well finish going through this book so I can give it back to the secretary. Wait a minute! I can't believe it. This looks perfect! Listen to this one: For rent: room in large, sunny home, close to campus for serious male student. Vegetarian, nonsmoker preferred: reasonable rent. I told you something would jump right out at me! What's the phone number? I've got to check this one out right away.

Sharon: It's 555-2387.

Fred: You've got to be kidding.

Sharon: Nope. That's the number, all right.

Fred: Do they give the address?

Sharon: Yup. 2367 Monterey Court.

Fred: Oh no! That's my address! That's where I'm living! I guess it isn't such a bad place after all. Come to think of it, I'd better go talk with the family I live with again before they rent out my room to someone else. See ya' later, OK?

Sharon: OK. Call me and tell me what happens.

Fred: I will. 'Bye.

Sharon: 'Bye. See ya' later.

A Place to Rent

Postlistening/Reading Questions

> Answer in complete sentences.

1. Why does Fred want to move?

   _____

2. Where does Sharon tell Fred to look for rentals?

   _____

3. Why does Sharon want to go to the campus housing office?

   _____

4. What does the housing office secretary give Fred?

   _____

5. Why do so many people want female roommates?

   _____

6. What part of the newspaper has rental information?

   _____

7. Where is the bulletin board on campus?

   _____

Vocabulary Building Sentences

> First, underline the word or expression from the vocabulary list in the prelistening/reading section. Then write a new sentence, using the same word or expression. Follow the model.

MODEL: My little brother is so <u>rowdy</u> that I can never get any studying done when he's around.

That was the rowdiest party I've ever been to.

1. I feel funny about going to the dance alone.

   _____

2. Offhand, I don't have any idea what kind of a grade I'm getting.

   _____

3. Be sure that you take down all the information the doctor gives you.

_____

4. I'm all set for my vacation. Are you?

_____

5. Here we go again! It seems like all they serve is spaghetti in this cafeteria.

_____

6. He always has the same old story to tell—he couldn't do his homework because he was too busy.

_____

7. That car jumped right out at me! I thought it was going to hit me.

_____

8. I wanted to try eating escargots, but I just couldn't handle it.

_____

9. Western movies are off my list. I'm really tired of them.

_____

10. I don't know whether I can win the award or not, but it's worth a shot.

_____

11. You've got to be kidding! You're not really going to France this summer, are you?

_____

12. I came too late. I should have known that the good stuff would go right away.

_____

13. He's such a slob. He always talks when he's got food in his mouth.

_____

14. I took down his phone number, but I lost it on the way home.

_____

15. I don't know if it's a good idea; I'll have to check it out.

_____

A Place to Rent

Word Forms

Complete the following sentences with the correct word form.

sensible   sensibly

1. I wish she would behave more _____

2. I would love to buy a Porsche, but I have to be _____

discriminate   discrimination   discriminatory

1. _____ in hiring practices is illegal.

2. Some people _____ against men because they think that women can do a better job.

3. His _____ remarks really bother me.

positive   positively

1. She usually thinks very _____ about others.

2. She has a _____ attitude.

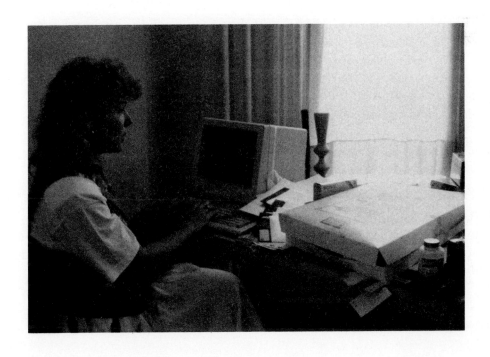

Conversation Activities

> Working in groups, discuss the following:

Do you think it's harder for a man to find a place to rent than it is for a woman? Is it a good idea for men and women who are not married to live in the same house with other unmarried people? If you needed a place to rent, where would you find information? How old do you think young people should be when they move out of their parents' house? Should men and women have the same freedom of choice? What are the advantages for students of sharing housing with other students? What are some of the disadvantages for students of sharing housing with other students?

Suggested Role-Plays

> Working in groups or in pairs, prepare a dialogue to share with the class. The following topics are suggestions for you to use.

1. **Participants: Anita, her roommates Nancy and Richard, and Anita's mother**
   Anita has just moved into an apartment with her friends Nancy and Richard. She hasn't told her mother that one of her new roommates is male, because she's afraid her mother would get angry and make her come home to live.

   Nancy: Whew! I'm glad we finished all of the grocery shoping for this week. That's a job I really hate to do.

   Anita: Me too, but I'd rather grocery shop than wash the kitchen floor and do the dishes.

   Nancy: Yeah! I can't believe that Richard said he'd wash the floors and do all of the dishes if we went shopping. He looked pretty cute wearing that apron and pushing that mop, didn't he? Well, here we are. Hey, were you expecting company? Whose car is that in front of the apartment?

   Anita: Oh my gosh! It's my mother's car!

   Finish the dialogue.

2. **Participants: John, his friend Sharon, and an apartment house manager**
   John has found an apartment he likes, and it is close to school. The manager of the apartment is not sure that he wants to rent to another student. The students who just moved out had loud parties and played rock music late every night.

   John: I'd like to see the one-bedroom apartment you have advertised.

   Manager: Is it for the two of you?

Sharon: No. I won't be living here. It's just for my friend, John.

Manager: Are you a student? I don't know if I want to rent to students again. I've had some pretty bad experiences.

Finish the dialogue.

Listening Comprehension Cloze Passage

> Listen to the tape of the following passage or to your teacher. Fill in the missing words as you hear them.

Of course, it depends on _____ 1 you want to live, but in most cities and even smaller _____ 2 , it is getting more and _____ 3 difficult to find inexpensive housing. For several years now it has been almost _____ 4 for young, first-time buyers to get _____ 5 money together to be able to _____ 6 their own home. As prices _____ 7 to climb, _____ 8 _____ 9 continue to go up.

People have had to learn to be more _____ 10 . Many young families who have been priced right out of the home market are now _____ 11 money from their parents and _____ 12 relatives so that they can meet the high down payment _____ 13 to buy their own homes.

Another answer is for two or _____ 14 families to buy a first home together. They put _____ 15 money together, and with their shared incomes, they _____ 16 one house and share the living space. Sometimes _____ 17 cook and eat together, and other times they _____ 18 the house into completely separate living units. _____ 19 several years of homeownership, they can sell the house and divide the _____ 20 . With the divided profit, each family is in a better _____ 21 to buy a separate house.

Another _____ is to buy a "fixer-upper." A fixer-upper is a
                    22

_____ that needs a lot of work. Sometimes that work is cosmetic, but
        23

_____ of the time if the price of the house is low, the work is
        24

_____. It may need a new roof, a new foundation, new floors, cabinets,
        25

electrical _____, or plumbing. If the buyers are willing to _____ in
                    26   27

a house that is almost _____ in a state of being remodeled, a fixer-upper may be
                            28

a _____ expensive way of getting into a home of their own.
        29

_____ _____ _____, it is getting to be a bigger
        30   31   32

and _____ challenge for those who want to share in the _____
        33   34

American dream of owning their own homes to think of _____
                                                              35

to make that dream possible.

Final Project

1. Talk with other students about your favorite room. Is it light and sunny, or is it dark and cool? Decribe what is in the room. Why is it your favorite room?
2. Discuss how you would feel if you shared a house with other families who were not related to you.
3. Describe what would be your perfect place to live.

9

At the Movies

General Warm-Up Questions

Read the following questions before you begin. They will help you to focus on the topic covered in this chapter.

Do you like to go to movies? What kinds of movies do you like? Do you ever see the same movie more than once? If so, how many times and which movie? Whom do you like to go to movies with? If you want to see one movie and your friend wants to see something else, who wins? How much does it cost to go to a movie? Does it cost more or less in different places?

Prelistening/Reading Study Questions

Read the following questions before you listen to or read the dialogue. Take a few moments to think about them. They will help you understand the dialogue when you begin.

Why doesn't Sharon want to see the film? How can Fred and Sharon find out what time the movie starts? What time do they go to the show? How much does it cost for each of them to go to the movie? Where do they go after the movie? Why does Fred like the film?

Vocabulary

BOMB: something unsuccessful with the public (usually a movie, a play, or another kind of performance)

TO TAKE IN: to go somewhere, to see something

TO GIVE SOMEONE A BREAK: to consider someone's thoughts or ideas

BEFORE MY TIME: before I was born, before I knew about something or understood it

TO DRAG SOMEONE SOMEWHERE: to take someone somewhere he or she really doesn't want to go

TO MIND SOMETHING: to object to, to be mildly against something

TO CUT IT OUT: to stop talking

TO CLEAN UP: to make a lot of money

JUNK: something that has no value to someone

BUCKS: dollars

CRITIC: someone who is paid to write about movies, plays, or art

FEATURE: showing; sometimes there are two features for one price (two movies)

FILM: movie

GRAB A . . . : to stop for a cup of coffee, soda, sandwich, quick meal, and so forth

HORROR: terror, fright, great fear; movies that are made intentionally to scare the audience

I'LL HAVE YOU KNOW THAT: I want you to know that . . . (used for emphasis)

I TOLD YOU SO: a reminder from someone that you didn't take his or her advice

NAH: no (This is common in fast, casual speech. When you are writing, it should always be written as *no*.)

TO RAKE IT IN: to make a lot of money (A mint is a place where the government takes paper and metals to produce coins and currency.)

MATINEE: an afternoon showing (sometimes it's less expensive)

OFFHAND: something that comes into your mind casually; without careful thought or consideration

GONNA: going to (This expression is common in fast, casual speech. When you are writing, it should always be as *going to*.)

TO HAVE SOMEONE'S NUMBER: to understand someone, to have him or her figured out, to know a person's likes or dislikes

FOXY: physically attractive; sexy

A STAR: a famous person in the world of entertainment; a way of ranking movies (one star is bad, two stars is fair, three stars is good, four stars is excellent)

PLOT: the story line in a play, movie, or book

PREVIEWS: short films that are advertisements for movies that will play at that theater in the future (also called *trailers*)

HOSTESS TWINKIES®:   a brand name for small, packaged cakes

REVIEW: a short critical article or discussion

SCREEN: the large white area on which movies are shown

SUBTITLES: translated dialogue at the bottom of the screen in foreign film

TRASHY: cheap; something that has no significant value

WEIRD: strange, unusual, unexplainable, disturbing

WHADDAYA WANT: what do you want?

'EM: them (This expression is common in fast, casual speech. When you are writing, it should be written as *them*.)

WINNER: something or someone successful

 AT THE MOVIES

Fred: Hey, I feel like doing something. Let's take in a movie.

Sharon: I don't know if I feel like it.

Fred: Come on. there's a great horror film playing at the Rio—it's called *The Monster That Ate Chicago*.

Sharon: Give me a break. I read a review of it in the paper. The critic says it's a bomb.

Fred: So? Who listens to critics?

Sharon: I think you should, a little more often.

Fred:	Waddaya mean?
Sharon:	Listen, you haven't picked a winner since *Gone with the Wind* first came out.
Fred:	Aren't you exaggerating a little? *Gone with the Wind* first came out in 1939—that was before my time.
Sharon:	Tell me, why are you always dragging me to these trashy movies?
Fred:	Sometimes I just feel like being entertained—like tonight. But you know, I like some serious films, too. I don't even mind foreign films with subtitles.
Sharon:	Do you know anyone who's seen *The Monster That Age Chicago*?
Fred:	Yeah. David and Janet saw it. They said it was great.
Sharon:	Hmmm. . . . Well, I do trust their judgment. All right, I'll go, but I get to pick the next movie we see.
Fred:	Yeah, yeah. You'll like *The Monster That Ate Chicago*, trust me.
Sharon:	What time does it start?
Fred:	I don't know offhand, but we can call the theater.
Sharon:	I'd rather buy a paper. Usually when you call the theater, you get a recorded voice on a tape. I don't like talking to machines.

(They buy a paper)

Fred:	Ah, here it is. It starts at seven.
Sharon:	Is there a second feature?
Fred:	Nope, just *The Monster That Ate Chicago*—but we can see it at bargain matinee prices if we go early enough.
Sharon:	I really think we'll be too late for the bargain matinee.
Fred:	I'm pretty sure we can make it. Trust me.
Sharon:	My mother used to say, "Never trust anyone who says: 'Trust me.'" I'm not so sure I believe you.

(At the movies)

Fred:	With four screens, I'll bet they really clean up here.
Sharon:	Yeah, I'm sure they rake it in, and for showing junk like this.
Fred:	Will you cut it out, Sharon? All you've been doing is complaining.

(At the ticket window)

Fred:	Two adults, please.
Ticket giver:	That'll be 12 dollars.
Fred:	Twelve bucks? The sign says four dollars each!
Ticket giver:	That's for the bargain matinee, sir. You're too late. It's after five.
Fred:	Oh well, it's only money. OK, two please.
Ticket giver:	That's screen number two, on your right.
Fred:	Thank you.
Sharon:	Yeah. It's only money. It's not her money, it's our money. I don't want to say I told you so . . . .
Fred:	But you told me so, right?

Sharon: Shhh . . . . It looks like it's already started.

Fred: Nah, these are just the previews.

(Sitting down)

Sharon: I wish they still had cartoons. I really miss the cartoons. Why do the tallest people always sit in front of me?

Fred: Shhh . . . stop complaining. It's too late to move now; there are no seats left and the movie's about to start. Look! That guy next to me just lit up a cigarette. That really drives me crazy. I'm going to talk to him. Excuse me sir, but there's no smoking allowed in this theater, so would you mind putting that out? Thank you.

Sharon: I forgot to buy popcorn. All I've got is this old package of Hostess Twinkies® I've been carrying around in my purse all day.

Fred: Well, don't go now. The movie's gonna start.

Sharon: What's a movie without popcorn? What'll you have?

Fred: Oh, OK, get me a medium with butter. Hurry back. You don't want to miss the beginning.

Sharon: Yeah, sure. I couldn't live if I missed the beginning of *The Monster That Age Chicago*.

Fred: Shhh . . . .

(Later)

Fred: Well, whaddaya think? Did you like the movie?

Sharon: I wouldn't even give it one star.

Fred: Personally, I liked the plot, the camera work, and the acting.

Sharon: Don't forget the lead actress. *She* is why you liked the movie. I've got your number.

Fred: Well, yeah—I liked her, too.

Sharon: You're lucky. There were no foxy men anywhere. All I had to look at was the monster.

Fred: Wanna grab a cup of coffee?

Sharon: OK, but I don't want to talk about that stupid movie. I can't believe that David and Janet actually liked it.

Fred: They did. Trust me. Well, I did promise you could pick the next one, right?

Sharon: Right. By the way, I like Ingmar Bergman films. How about you?

Fred: You mean that Swedish director who does all those weird subtitled movies?

Sharon: He's the one. But his movies aren't weird. I like 'em a lot.

Fred: Hey, look at this sign: "Coming next week: *Bambi Meets Godzilla*."

Sharon: Oh no! Not again! Gimme a break!

Postlistening/Reading Questions

> Answer in complete sentences.

1. Why doesn't Sharon want to see the film?

_____

2. How can you find out what time a movie starts?

_____

3. Do Sharon and Fred go to the movies early enough for the bargain matinee?

_____

4. How much does it cost for each of them to go to the movie?

_____

5. Where do they go after the movie?

_____

6. What does Fred like about the movie?

_____

Vocabulary Building Sentences

> First, underline the word or expression from the vocabulary list in the prelistening/reading section. Then write a new sentence, using the same word or expression. Follow the model.

MODEL: I'd like to take in that new art exhibit, but I don't have the time.

David said he'd like to take in a concert next weekend, but I'd rather go to the beach.

1. I wish he'd give us a break. We've all worked very hard.

_____

2. I don't remember the Cuban Missle Crisis. That was before my time.

_____

3. Why do you always drag me to these dances? You know I don't like to dance.

_____

At the Movies

4. We should open a Mexican restaurant on campus. We could really clean up!

   _____

5. Sure, I'll go to the cafeteria with you. I've just got enough time to grab a quick cup of coffee.

   _____

6. I heard that my neighbors really raked it in when they sold their house.

   _____

7. The film *Heaven's Gate* was one of Hollywood's biggest bombs.

   _____

8. I'd tell you the answer, but I don't know it offhand.

   _____

9. I hear they lost big bucks when they went to Las Vegas.

   _____

10. Would you mind closing the window? I'm freezing.

    _____

11. Janet always says she doesn't have enough money when I know she does. I've got her number.

    _____

12. Come on, little brother, cut it out! Just leave me alone for a while, will you? I'm trying to study.

    _____

Word Forms

Complete the following sentences with the correct word form.

critic   criticize   critical

1. She's a very _____ person.

2. I read Janet's articles; she's a good _____

3. Don't _____ me. I'm doing the best that I can.

horrifying   horror   horrified

1. I was _____ when I heard about the accident. I almost went with them!

2. The thought of nuclear war is _____

3. The first _____ movie I ever saw was *Frankenstein and the Wolf-man*.

act   actor   actresses

1. I like Jane Fonda; she can really _____

2. I think Robert DeNiro is a great _____

3. Katharine Hepburn, who has been in films since the 1920s, is one of the world's greatest

_____ .

fox   foxy   foxiest

1. My neighbor is the _____ woman I've ever seen.

2. The _____ who used to live across the street moved out last week.

3. I would like to meet a _____ looking man.

Conversation Activities

Working in groups, discuss the following:

What kinds of movies do you like? Have you ever seen a foreign film? If you have, which one have you seen? What is the title of your favorite movie? Who is your favorite movie star? Did you ever go to a movie that scared you? What was the title? How often do you go to the movies? If you could play a part in any movie, what movie would it be in, and what part would you play?

Suggested Role-Play

Working in groups or in pairs, prepare a dialogue to share with the class. The following topics are suggestions for you to use.

1. **Participants: Alice, Mary, Jennifer, a famous movie star, and his agent**
   Alice, Mary, and Jennifer are sitting in a small restaurant when a well-known movie star comes in to sit quietly and drink a cup of coffee.

Alice:	Well, what are you going to order?
Mary:	I don't know. Maybe I'll just have a cup of tea. I'm pretty broke this month.
Jennifer:	Me, too. I think I'll just have some coffee.
Alice:	Boy. This has turned out to be a boring evening. Nothing exciting ever happens in this town.
Mary:	Who's that guy with the dark glasses on who just sat down in the corner over there? He looks familiar.
Jennifer:	Wait a minute! That's Tom Hanks!
Alice:	You're kidding.
Jennifer:	No, I know it's Tom Hanks! I just saw him in a movie two days ago.
Mary:	I think you're right. It *is* Tom Hanks. Who's got the courage to go over and talk to him?
Alice:	Not me. No way. You go, Jennifer. You're the one who recognized him.

   Finish the dialogue.

2. **Participants: Two famous movie stars**
   They have all of the material things they could ever want, but they can't think of anything exciting to do.

Star 1:	I don't know what to do this summer. My life is so boring.
Star 2:	I know what you mean. I think I've been everywhere in the world either on location or on vacation.
Star 1:	Why don't you go to that lovely house you have in the south of France, the one your fifth husband gave to you as a wedding present?
Star 2:	We were just there two years ago.
Star 1:	There's always your Manhattan penthouse.
Star 2:	It's too hot in New York in the summer, and I don't really like the servants at the penthouse.
Star 1:	You could always come with us. We're going to do something *very* different this summer.
Star 2:	Oh! What is it?

   Finish the dialogue.

At the Movies

Listening Comprehension Cloze Passage

> Listen to the tape of the following passage or to your teacher. Fill in the missing words as you hear them.

_____ 1 of the greatest American movies that has ever been made is *Gone with the Wind*. Adapted from a _____ 2 by Margaret Mitchell, *Gone with the Wind* is _____ 3 epic. A romanticized account of the _____ 4 Civil War, the film is four _____ 5 long. The movie stars Clark Gable as Rhett Butler and Vivien Leigh _____ 6 Scarlett O'Hara. It won eight Academy Awards _____ 7 best director and best actress. The movie cost four million _____ 8 to produce. In 1939, that was a lot of _____ 9.

The movie was well into production and the director had screen-tested hundreds of women —_____ 10 of them very famous actresses—but had not found the right woman to play Scarlett O'Hara. Vivien Leigh came to _____ 11 movie set with her husband to _____ 12 the filming of the _____ 13 scene of the burning of Atlanta when the director saw her and decided that she _____ 14 be perfect to play the role _____ 15 Scarlett.

Clark Gable as Rhett Butler was the first _____ 16 to swear in a major motion picture. His last line in the _____ 17, "Frankly my dear, I don't give a damn," is still famous. _____ 18 one had ever said _____ 19 in a movie before.

Gone with the Wind has spectacular cinematography and _____ 20 very beautiful music. It is available on videocassette _____ 21 is almost as popular now as it

was _____ years ago. There are other famous films that were
        22

_____ in 1939 like *Wuthering Heights, Mr. Smith Goes to Washington, Goodbye, Mr.*
        23

Chips, _____ *The Wizard of Oz.* Along _____ *Gone with the Wind,*
                24   25

they will always remain the favorites. These films and others are now called classics.

_____ have memorized much of the dialogue, know all of the music, and can
        26

watch them _____ and again without _____ bored.
                  27   28

Final Project

1. Talk about the differences between watching something on television and watching something in a movie theater. Which is better? Why?

2. Discuss the different kinds of entertainment you enjoy doing with other people. Do you like to go to movies, concerts, sports, dances, picnics, and parties? Do you usually need money to enjoy yourself? What things do you like to do? Are the things that you like to do expensive?

3. There are some things we enjoy doing with others, and some things we like to do by ourselves. Think specifically of something that you like to do by yourself. Pretend that you have a lot of money and a lot of time, but that you have to be alone. Where are you? What are you doing?

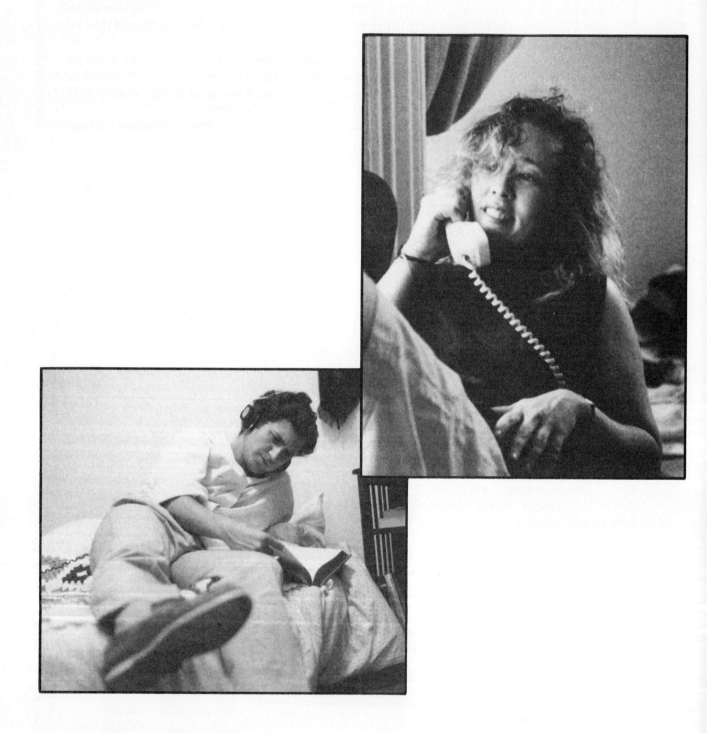

Fred's Date

General Warm-Up Questions

Read the following questions before you begin. They will help you to focus on the topic covered in this chapter.

Some people feel more comfortable when they go out with a group of people than they do when they are just with one person. Do you feel more comfortable when you go out with three or four people than when you go out with just one person? Where did you go on your first date? Have most of the dates you have had been arranged by friends or members of your family? A formal date is usually planned in advance and sometimes includes dinner, a concert or a dance. You often get dressed up for a formal date. Is formal dating more fun than informal dating? At what age should boys begin to date? Is the age the same for girls?

Prelistening/Reading Study Questions

Read the following questions before you listen to or read the dialogue. Take a few moments to think about them. They will help you understand the dialogue when you begin.

Fred says that he feels strange. Why does he feel strange? Where did he meet the blonde woman he talks about? Has Sharon gone out on inexpensive dates? If so, where has she gone? What does Sharon tell Fred not to forget? Where is he going on his big date? Why does Sharon think it's a good idea for women to ask men out on dates?

Vocabulary

TO BE GOING ON: to be happening; occurring

WEIRD: strange, unusual, unexplainable, disturbing

TO HANDLE (SOMETHING OR SOMEONE): to take care of, to deal with, to resolve

IT'D: it would (This is common in fast, casual speech. When you are writing, it should be written as *it would*.)

TO HAVE GOOD EARS: to be a good listener

A PAIN: something you do not want to do; a problem you don't want to face

TO PARTY: common noun that has recently gained acceptance as a verb; it is conjugated as a regular verb

TO GET CARRIED AWAY: to become involved in what you are doing (often so much that you forget other things)

SHOOT: go ahead; say what you want to say; used in conversation to mean "ask me" or "tell me"

D'YOU: do you (This is common in fast, casual speech. When you are writing, it should be written as *do you*.)

FOXY: physically attractive; sexy

TO GET UP THE COURAGE: to become brave enough to do something that is difficult

TO REJECT: to push someone or something away; to refuse

TO BE ALL SETTLED: to arrange something; to take care of something so it is no longer a problem

TO CHICKEN OUT: to decide not to do something because you are afraid of doing it

TO COME ON TOO STRONG: to present yourself in a forceful way, to push yourself on someone

WHAT'D: what did (This is common in fast, casual speech. When you are writing, it should be written as *what did*.)

A SHOCK: a surprise, something unexpected (can be good or bad)

DYNAMITE: something very good, great

TO BE LIBERATED: to be aware of your rights as a person

TO GO BROKE: to spend or use all of your money

TO GO DUTCH: each person pays for his or her share of the bill

TO BE RIDICULOUS: to be foolish; to be silly

TO DEAL WITH (SOMETHING OR SOMEONE): to take care of, to handle, to resolve

TO BE GRATEFUL: to be full of thanks; to appreciate someone or something

TAKE IT EASY: relax; calm down; don't worry

Fred's Date

Sharon: What's going on, Fred? You look weird today.

Fred: I don't know . . . it's really strange. Something happened the other night that I don't know how to handle.

Sharon: Well maybe it'd help to talk about it. I've got good ears.

Fred: OK. Remember that potluck at John's house where you made that great fruit salad?

Sharon: How could I forget. That's the night I didn't get home until two, and then I had to study until four-thirty. What a pain. I like to go out, but sometimes it's just not worth it when I've got a lot of studying to do and I have to work hard to catch up for all the time I've lost partying.

Fred: I thought you just said you had good ears. Do you want to hear what happened to me or not?

Sharon: Sure. I'm sorry. I just got carried away for a minute. Shoot. I won't interrupt. I promise.

Fred: Well. D'you remember that foxy blonde who was sitting next to Jeff most of the evening?

Sharon: Yeah, I think so. The tall one with green eyes?

Fred: That's the one. It took me more than an hour to get up the courage to go over and talk to her. I tried to think of some way to ask for her phone number, but I chickened out. I was afraid she'd think I was coming on too strong if I just said, "Say, I'd like to call you up sometime."

Sharon: I know. It can be very hard . . . especially when it's someone you really like. We're all afraid of rejection.

Fred: Well. Anyhow, listen to this. Last night she called and asked me out on a date. Isn't that a surprise?

Sharon: No kidding! Really?

Fred: Of course, really. Would I lie?

Sharon: Well? Tell me, tell me, what'd you say?

Fred: After I got over the initial shock, I said yes, of course.

Sharon: So? Then it's all settled. What are you worried about?

Fred: The problem is that I don't know what to do now. I've never been asked out on a date before. Isn't it unusual for a woman to ask a man out on a date?

Sharon: Not anymore. I think it's a dynamite idea. Think of all the years I wasted sitting next to the phone waiting to be asked out. If I had been more liberated, I think I would have asked guys out all the time.

Fred: Yeah, sure. You would have gone broke, too. It can be very expensive to take someone out.

Sharon: Aw, come on. Some of the best dates I've had have been very inexpensive. I've gone on picnics, for walks on the beach, to the zoo, to potlucks, poetry readings, and to play baseball, just to name a few. I think it's a lot more fun to think of things to do without spending money. You just have to be a little more creative. If she's asked you out, you shouldn't have to worry about paying anyway.

Fred: You're kidding? Really?

Sharon: Of course, really. Would I lie?

Fred: You mean she'll pay for the date?

Sharon: It'd probably be a good idea to talk about it before you got out and be sure you're prepared to pay for your half just in case she wants to go Dutch.

Fred's Date

Fred: What do you mean, talk about it? How can I say, "Hey there, are you paying for me tonight?"

Sharon: No, don't be ridiculous.

Fred: I'm not being ridiculous. How do I deal with it? Do I just wait and then fight with her over the bill when it comes?

Sharon: I think that I'd offer to pay, just as if you were out with anyone else. Then, if she says something like, "I asked you out. I am paying the bill," just say thank you and be grateful. You can say something like, "Great. I'll pay the next time."

Fred: I don't think I will *ever* understand the new liberated woman.

Sharon: Hey, times are changing. You've got to take it easy, my friend. Oh, I almost forgot. Remember, we're all going to meet at the park to play baseball on Saturday afternoon. It should be a good game. By the way, where are you going on this big, fancy date, anyway?

Fred: To play baseball at the park on Saturday afternoon.

Sharon: No kidding? Really?

Fred: Would I lie?

Postlistening/Reading Questions

> Answer in complete sentences.

1. Why does Fred feel strange?

   _____

2. Where did he meet the blonde woman?

   _____

3. Why didn't Fred ask for her phone number?

   _____

4. Where has Sharon gone on inexpensive dates?

   _____

5. What does Sharon tell Fred not to forget?

   _____

6. Where is Fred going on his big date?

   _____

7. Does Sharon think that it is a good idea for women to ask men out on dates? Why? Why not?

   _____

Vocabulary Building Sentences

First, underline the word or expression from the vocabulary list in the prelistening/reading section. Then write a new sentence, using the same word or expression. Follow the model.

MODEL: What's <u>going on</u>? I thought you'd be here an hour ago.

Their relationship's been going on for a long time.

1. I always feel weird after an exam.

   _____

2. I can't handle any more problems today. Everything's gone wrong.

   _____

3. Janet spent a lot of money last week. Did she get carried away?

   _____

4. I want to hear about your trip. Shoot. I'm listening.

   _____

5. My brother got up the courage to apply to UCLA.

   _____

6. I wanted to go skiing, but I chickened out. I was afraid that I'd break a leg.

   _____

7. David and I went Dutch for lunch, so it wasn't too expensive.

   _____

8. It's all settled. Andy's having the party at his house.

   _____

9. Do you think I've been coming on too strong lately?

   _____

10. I'm saving my money. I don't want to go broke this month.

    _____

11. It's a big problem, but I'm sure you can deal with it.

_____

12. Why can't you just relax and take it easy?

_____

Word Forms

> Complete the following sentences with the correct word form.

liberation   liberate   liberated

1. The American troops helped _____ France at the end of World War II.

2. The Women's _____ movement began many years before the 1960s.

3. I felt _____ after the exams.

party   partied   partying

1. I _____ all night last night. That's why I'm so tired today.

2. John's _____ was a lot of fun.

3. I didn't get all of my homework done because we were _____ at the beach yesterday.

ridiculous   ridiculously

1. That math class is _____ easy for me. But then my father's a math teacher.

2. I wish he would wipe that _____ smile off his face.

Fred's Date

grateful   gratitude   gratefully

1. She was _____ to her grandmother for teaching her to fight for what she believed in.

2. I accepted the money _____

3. I have nothing but _____ to my friend for his help.

foxy   foxiest   foxier

1. Paul Newman is _____ than my husband.

2. That's a _____ new hairdo you've got.

3. Fred said that the woman he took to the baseball game was the

_____ woman he's ever met.

Conversation Activities

Working in groups, discuss the following:

In the United States, some women feel comfortable asking men out on dates, but it's still difficult for many women to ask a man out. Is it common in your native country for a woman to ask a man out on a date? If a woman asks a man out, should she choose where they will go and what they will do? If a woman asks a man out, should she pay for everything? Do you think that it is important to spend a lot of money if you want to impress someone? Is it hard for you to say no to someone who asks you out? When do you pay your own way when you go out with someone? If you are a man, what would you do if a woman offered to pay for herself? If you are a woman, when would you offer to share the bill with your date? Have you ever been to a really great party? Where and when was it?

Suggested Role-Plays

Working in groups or in pairs, prepare a dialogue to share with the class. The following topics are suggestions for you to use.

1. **Participants: Andrew, Susan, and an airline ticket agent**
   Andrew forgot to make plane reservations, and there are no seats left. His brother's getting married, and both he and his brother need to get to Chicago. It is too late to drive or go by train.

Andrew:	My brother's getting married tomorrow morning. It's going to be a fancy garden wedding. He's starting to get very nervous.
Susan:	Wow. I guess. I'd be nervous, too. Where's the wedding?
Andrew:	It's in Chicago at his fiancée's parents' house. But he's still here finishing up all of his exams.
Susan:	When's he leaving for Chicago?
Andrew:	We're both leaving in just a few hours. I've got to go pick him up. We're taking the last flight out tonight. It'll get us there just in time for the wedding.
Susan:	It's a good thing you've already got your airplane tickets. Everything's booked solid this time of year.
Andrew:	Tickets!? Oh no! I was supposed to get our tickets! Can I use your phone?

Finish the dialogue.

2. Participants: Jennifer, David, and the waiter

Jennifer and David are on a date. They are having dinner at a very elegant, expensive restaurant. He doesn't know it yet, but when David takes out his wallet to pay the bill, he will find a note from his brother that says: "I borrowed 25 dollars. Thanks. I'll pay you back tomorrow. Michael." David does not have enough money left to pay the bill. Jennifer has just three dollars in her purse.

Jennifer:	What a wonderful dinner! I'd never had Australian lobster tail before. They were wonderful!
David:	I'm glad that you liked them. My salmon Wellington was good, too.
Jennifer:	This was such an extravagance! You shouldn't have taken me to such a fancy restaurant, David. We could have gone out for pizza or hamburgers.
David:	No way! You're birthday only happens once a year. I wanted to take you to someplace very special. Waiter, check please.

Finish the dialogue.

Listening Comprehension Cloze Passage

> Listen to the tape of the following passage or to your teacher. Fill in the missing words as you hear them.

The ritual of dating _____ the United States has gone _____
1   2
many changes in the last 30 years.

During the 1950s, _____ was very traditional. Men did all of the asking
3
out, _____ all the expenses and, most of the time, chose where to go. Before
4
a man _____ a woman on the phone to ask her out, he had _____
5   6
decided where they would go and what they would do. It was not socially

110   Fred's Date

_____ for a woman to call a man, so _____ spent a lot of time
      7   8

waiting by _____ phones. Often a first date was a _____ date with
            9   10

two couples, but many dates were just for two.

   In the 1960s _____ into the 1970s came the youth movements. There was
                 11

_____ speech, a new interest in women's liberation, _____ against
   12   13

an unpopular war, and drugs. People didn't date as much. They did more

things together as groups than as couples. The dating that _____ go on was for
                                                             14

the most part much _____ formal than the dating of the 1950s.
                    15

_____ was less planning and more spontaneity, and many social
   16

_____ were planned by both men and _____. People *got*
   17   18

together more than *went out on dates*. The very word *date* seemed to _____
                                                                          19

from our culture for a while.

   As the 1980s _____, things began to swing back _____ again.
                 20   21

Traditional dating became more _____, and group activities became less the
                                22

norm. Dating seems to be more _____ today than it was in the 1960s and 1970s.
                               23

Even women's clothes today look more _____ what was popular in the 1950s. It
                                      24

is _____ that the women of _____ are more willing to pay their
   25   26

own way and are more likely to _____ a man out on a date _____
                                27   28

their sisters in the 1950s. Perhaps we will _____ return to those days when
                                             29

women relied entirely on men to make the _____. Do you think that
                                          30

would be good?

Final Project

> 1. Talk about the best date you have ever had. Where did you go and what did you do?
> 2. Have you ever been on a blind date? If you have, discuss your experience.
> 3. Think of someone you know who has a perfect marriage or relationship. What do you think makes it perfect?

11

The Part-Time Job

General Warm-Up Questions

Read the following questions before you begin. They will help you to focus on the topic covered in this chapter.

If you could have any job, anywhere in the world, what would it be? What would be the worst job you could have? Would you like to do the same work your father or your mother did? How old should people be before they begin to work? Should they have jobs when they are still in school?

Prelistening/Reading Study Questions

Read the following questions before you listen to or read the dialogue. Take a few moments to think about them. They will help you understand the dialogue when you begin.

Why has Fred decided not to take chemistry? When does Fred want to work? Where is the Student Job Placement Office? What does the job placement secretary ask to see? How late is the Student Job Placement Office open? Why doesn't Fred want a job taking care of children?

Vocabulary

TO RUN OUT OF: not to have any more of something

YA': you (This expression is common in fast, casual speech. When you are writing, it should be written as *you*.)

IT'D: it would (This is common in fast, casual speech. It should be written as *it would*.)

D'YA: do you (This is common in fast, casual speech. When you are writing, these words should always be written as *do you*.)

GONNA: going to (This pronunciation is common in fast, casual speech. When you are writing, it should always be written as *going to*.)

TO EXPECT: to think that something is going to happen; to wait for something you expect will come

TO BE HARD ON SOMEONE: to be strict with; to be difficult

TO BE BALD: not to have hair on your head; not to have tread on tires

TO PAY ATTENTION TO: to notice

WHADDAYA: what do you

TO BE TIGHT ABOUT SOMETHING: to be strict; to be conservative with money

WAGES: money earned by working

RIGHT UP ONE'S ALLEY: what one likes to do, or does well

TO TAKE OFF: to leave

TO STRUGGLE THROUGH: to fight with; to work very hard for or at something

AWFUL: terrible, very bad

TO CHECK INTO: to study something, to look into something

NO WAY: (slang) impossible

TOUGH: difficult, unfortunate

OUT OF LUCK: unlucky

DON'T GET ME WRONG: don't misunderstand me

TO DROP OUT OF: to stop attending an activity; to stop belonging to a group

YOU'D: you would (This pronunciation is common in fast, casual speech.)

ARRANGE: to plan; to put in order

TO TAKE A LOOK AT: to investigate, to consider, to examine something

GOTTA: (have) got to (This pronunciation is common in fast, casual speech. When you are writing, it should be written as *got to*.)

TO GIVE SOMEONE A BREAK: to give someone a chance; to make things easier for that person

NO KIDDING: really? is that true?

THERE'RE: there are (This pronunciation is common in fast, casual speech.)

TO GET TO BE: to become

NAH: no (This is common in fast, casual speech. In writing, it should be *no*.)

TO SHOW SOMEONE AROUND: to help make someone feel more comfortable by helping them learn about something

IN THE MEANTIME: for now; until something else happens

WANNA: want to (This pronunciation is common in fast, casual speech. When you are writing, it should be written as *want to*.)

PROOF: information that shows something is true; evidence

TO PRESENT A GOOD IMAGE: to make people think well of you; to make a good impression

FIRMLY: strongly (but not too strongly)

TO WORK OUT: to happen to someone's advantage; to happen the way you want something to happen

 ## THE PART-TIME JOB

Sharon: Hi there, Fred. Good to see ya' back! Are you ready for this semester?

Fred: I'm never ready for a new semester. I've still gotta buy my books, and the line at the bookstore is awful.

Sharon: You'd better hurry and get your chemistry book before they run out. I hear there're a lot more people in the class than they expected.

The Part-Time Job

Fred: I'm not taking chemistry this semester.

Sharon: No kidding, why not?

Fred: The lab meets in the afternoon, and I've gotta find a job.

Sharon: I think there must be times when people choose careers because of their class schedules. My friend Bill became an engineer because all the engineering classes met on Tuesdays and Thursdays. Are you gonna have to drop out of school?

Fred: No way. I've worked it out so all my classes are in the morning. That way I'll have my afternoons free to work.

Sharon: Isn't that gonna be hard on you? If you go to school all morning and work all afternoon, you won't have much time or energy left to study.

Fred: I don't have any choice. My utility bill just went up again, my rent went up, and I need new tires for my car. The ones I have now are almost completely bald.

Sharon: That sounds tough. Where ya' gonna look for a job?

Fred: I thought I'd check into the Student Job Placement Office here on campus first.

Sharon: I've never been there. Where is it?

Fred: It's downstairs right across from the cafeteria. Haven't you seen the sign? There's a sign that says "Student Job Placement Office" right on the side of the building.

Sharon: Yeah, I guess so, but I never really paid any attention to it. Maybe I'll go with you. It'd be nice to have a little extra money. Can anyone go in to ask them about jobs?

Fred: Sure. They have a few rules, though. They'll help you find a job if you're enrolled in classes now, or if you used to be a student.

Sharon: When are you goin' to the Student Job Placement Office?

Fred: I think I'll go there now. D'ya wanna come?

Sharon: Yeah. I'd like to see what this is all about.

(In the Job Placement Office)

Secretary: Can I help you with something?

Fred: Yes, I'm looking for a part-time job.

Secretary: Are you a student here?

Fred: I sure am.

Secretary: May I see your student ID?

Fred: Here it is.

Secretary: This card isn't punched for the current semester. Do you have your registration card?

Fred: I think it's here somewhere. Ah, yes. Here it is.

Secretary: This is fine. If you'll fill out this application, we can get started.

Sharon: Can I have one, too?

Secretary: May I see your student ID?

Sharon: I left it at home.

Secretary: Oh-oh. You'll have to come back when you have some proof of enrollment.

Sharon: No problem. I can come back tomorrow. How late are you open?

Secretary: We're open until four-thirty.

(A few minutes later)

Fred: OK. I've finished filling out this application. What do I do now?

The Part-Time Job

Secretary:	Take a look at the job board behind you. Each of the cards is for one job, and each of the cards has a number on it. If you see anything that looks interesting, write down the numbers on the cards and bring them to someone here at the counter. We can usually send you out on two job interviews a day.
Fred:	OK. Do all of them pay the same wages?
Secretary:	Most of them are right around minimum wage. Some pay a little higher. The only ones that pay lower are the child-care jobs.
Sharon:	Hey, Fred, take a look at this. Here's a job for a tour guide. All you'd have to do is show people around. That sounds like fun. Do you speak Hebrew?
Fred:	Hebrew? I have a hard enough time with English. Why?
Sharon:	That rules out that job. They want someone who speaks fluent Hebrew.
Fred:	See anything else interesting? Oh, look. Here's a section that says "Quick Cash." That's right up my alley. Hmmmm . . . Herbal Life Products. Sales position. I've never been very good at sales jobs. Have you found anything else?
Sharon:	There are a lot here under "Math" and "Engineering."
Fred:	No thanks, I have a hard enough time struggling through math myself.
Sharon:	How about doing some yard work? There are a lot of jobs for students who can do clean-up work.
Fred:	That sounds too much like physical labor. I get tired pretty easily.
Sharon:	Here's one for a driver. You'd drive a truck for a furniture company.
Fred:	Now you're talking. I've always wanted to drive a big truck. What's the number on the card?
Sharon:	It's number 18.
Fred:	Great! See anything else?
Sharon:	Nah. That seems to be about it, unless you want a child-care job.
Fred:	Give me a break. I have to take care of my little brother all the time. Don't get me wrong. It's not that I don't like kids, but I'd like to do something different for a change.
Sharon:	I can understand that.
Fred:	OK. I think I've found something. I'm interested in number 18—the truck driving job. What do I do now?
Secretary:	Let me look it up and find out where it is and what the hours are. Here we go. It's in the city. Is that OK with you?
Fred:	Yeah, that's perfect.
Secretary:	Let me call them and tell them I'm sending you out for an interview.
Fred:	OK, fine.
Secretary:	Can you be there tomorrow at one o'clock?
Fred:	Sure. Is there anything else I should know about the job or the interview?
Secretary:	Not really. Just be sure you're on time. Of course it's important that you're neatly dressed and clean, so you present a good image. Also make sure that you shake hands firmly. It's important that you appear confident and responsible. Because it's a driving job, they are going to want to check your driving record and make sure that you have a valid driver's license.
Fred:	OK. Thanks for the help. I've got a couple of friends who would probably like to get part-time jobs, too.
Secretary:	Just send them in. That's what we're here for.
Fred:	OK. I'll do that. They're international students. Will that make a difference?

The Part-Time Job

Secretary:	You mean they're here on student visas?
Fred:	Yeah, I think so.
Secretary:	That does make a difference. The Department of Immigration and Naturalization sets some pretty serious restrictions on foreign students. They are allowed to work part time, but only under special circumstances and usually with written permission from INS. I'm sure that someone in the international student's office can answer their questions.
Fred:	OK. I'll pass on the information. Thanks for all the help.
Secretary:	Anytime. Please come back and tell me what happens when you go out on that job interview. If that job doesn't work out, I'll be happy to help you find something else if I can. Also, you know that we have career planning classes and counselors who can help you prepare for job interviews as well as answer any questions you may have about the working world. We also have information about transferring to other colleges. Perhaps your international student friends would like to find out about our career planning classes. We can help them make decisions and prepare to go out in the working world. There are no restrictions with the classes or the counseling we offer.
Fred:	That's really good to know. When I get ready to start making decisions, I'll check with you first.
Sharon:	Hey Fred, I'm going to take off now. I have to get to class. See ya' later in the cafeteria, OK?
Fred:	Sure, see ya'.
Sharon:	Let me know how it works out with the job.
Fred:	OK, see you later.
Sharon:	OK. Bye.

Postlistening/Reading Questions

> Answer in complete sentences.

1. Why has Fred decided not to take chemistry?

   _____

2. When does Fred want to work?

   _____

3. Where is the Student Job Placement Office?

   _____

4. What does the Student Job Placement secretary ask to see?

   _____

5. How late is the Student Job Placement Office open?

   _____

6. Why can't Fred take the job as a tour guide?

_____

7. Why doesn't Fred want a job taking care of children?

_____

8. What do foreign students need in order to get part-time jobs?

_____

Vocabulary Building Sentences

First, underline the word or expression from the vocabulary list in the prelistening/reading section. Then write a new sentence, using the same word or expression. Follow the model.

MODEL: Give me a call when you get here. I'll <u>show you around.</u>

It's nice to have someone show you around when you're in a new place.

1. He always runs out of money before the end of the month.

_____

2. My father was always hard on me when I was growing up.

_____

3. My physics teacher is very tight on deadlines. She won't accept any late papers.

_____

4. Do you have to take off so soon? I was hoping you could stay for dinner.

_____

5. If history is right up your alley, you can help me study for my final exam!

_____

6. Give me a break! I've already got too much to do. I can't take your books back to the library.

_____

7. My girlfriend wants to break up, but I'm hoping we can work out our problems.

_____

8. My brother had to check into the hospital last week.

_____

9. It seems like everything is going up these days. I have trouble paying all of my bills.

_____

10. Don't get me wrong. I do want to go out with you; I just don't have the time.

_____

11. Let me take a look at your paper. Maybe I can help you with it.

_____

Word Forms

Complete the following sentences with the correct word form.

expected   expect   expecting

1. My sister is _____ her first baby next month.

2. My parents _____ us to be on time for dinner.

3. If you _____ to get an A in your English class, you will have to work very hard.

proof   proven   prove

1. In order to use the Student Job Placement Office's services, you must

_____ that you are or have been a student.

2. Your registration receipt is _____ that you are a student.

3. Once you have _____ your student status, the Student Job Placement Office can help you.

arrangements   arrange   arranges

1. My brother always _____ his time carefully.

2. What kind of _____ have you made for the summer?

3. I have to _____ my schedule of classes next semester so that I will have lots of time to study.

Conversation Activities

Working in groups, discuss the following:

If you could work anywhere in the world, where would it be? What kind of job would you have? Do you think that it's hard to find a good job? How would you present a good image if you were looking for a job? What is the worst job you have ever had? How long did you have it? Do you think it is easier for a man to get a job than a woman?

Suggested Role-Plays

Working in groups or in pairs, prepare a dialogue to share with the class. The following topics are suggestions for you to use.

1. **Participants: Fred and Mr. Davis, the owner of the trucking company**
   Fred has come to the office of Acme Trucking Company to apply for a part-time job.

   Fred: Hello, my name is Fred Jones. I'm here to apply for the job as truck driver.
   Mr. Davis: Oh yeah, you're from the college?
   Fred: Yes, sir. I am.
   Mr. Davis: Great. They called and said you were coming. Come on in and sit down. I'll be right with you as soon as I get this order out.
   Fred: Thank you, sir.
   Mr. Davis: OK. Now tell me about yourself.

   Finish the dialogue.

2. **Participants: Mrs. Andrews and the Job Placement Office Secretary (on the phone)**
   Mrs. Andrews can't find anyone to take care of her children in the afternoon.

   Mrs. Andrews: Hello. This is Janet Andrews. I understand that you have students who are looking for part-time jobs.
   Secretary: Yes, we do. Are you interested in hiring a student?
   Mrs. Andrews: I sure am. I've been trying to find someone for more than a month. The last three people I hired only stayed a day or two.
   Secretary: I don't understand. Is there a problem with the job?
   Mrs. Andrews: No, not really. It's just taking care of my children in the afternoon for a few hours.
   Secretary: That sounds reasonable. I don't understand what the problem has been.
   Mrs. Andrews: Well, I've got 11 children.

   Finish the dialogue.

Listening Comprehension Cloze Passage

> Listen to the tape of the following passage or to your teacher. Fill in the missing words as you hear them.

Many students work _____ 1 time while they are going to school. As _____ 2 becomes more and more expensive, students need to subsidize the costs of _____ 3 housing, books, and tuition with additional money from extra _____ 4 .

Often, students can find jobs on _____ 5 in the cafeteria, coffee shop, bookstore, snack bar, library, and offices. There are _____ 6 places on campus where students can find work. If they _____ 7 to work with other students and are very _____ 8 in certain subjects, they can often work as paid tutors in learning _____ 9 . All campuses utilize student assistants. It is _____ 10 for the students because it helps them _____ 11 their bills, and it is good for the campus _____ 12 they get inexpensive talented laborers.

It is also common _____ 13 students to work full time _____ 14 the summer or at other times when school is not in session. During the holiday _____ 15 , it is always fairly _____ 16 to find jobs in retail because all of the stores are busy preparing for _____ 17 of shoppers. There are many jobs for students in the service _____ 18 such as retail sales and food service.

Some students are fortunate enough to find jobs in the _____ 19 they are studying. _____ 20 someone who wants to become a teacher can find a job _____ 21 as a teacher's aide. People who want to go into nursing or medicine _____ 22 often find jobs in _____ 23 or other health care facilities while they are still students. Students who are _____ 24 tourism or restaurant management can find jobs in hotels or _____ 25 . It is always helpful to be

_____ to work in your field while you are studying. Sometimes those jobs will
    26

help you _____ if you are really studying what _____ right for
            27   28

you. It's better to _____ your mind while you are still a student
                      29

_____ to change your mind when you have completed all of _____
  30   31

education.

Final Project

Write down five different jobs that interest you. Go to the local library and research them. Find out the following: where you would study; how much your education would cost; how long it would take to get the degree you would need to begin working; and how much money you could make.

12

The Assessment Test

General Warm-Up Questions

Read the following questions before you begin. They will help you to focus on the topic covered in this chapter.

Does it bother you when you know that you have to take a test? Do you get nervous? What was the most difficult test you ever had to take? Did you have to take a test to get a driver's license? Was the driver's test as bad as a test in school?

Prelistening/Reading Study Questions

Read the following questions before you listen to or read the dialogue. Take a few moments to think about them. They will help you understand the dialogue when you begin.

Where did Fred go during the summer? Why is he on campus early? Where is María Luz from? What is she worried about? Why does Sharon want to go to the bookstore early? Why does María Luz need to take the assessment? What kind of a job does María Luz have in Colombia? How can an ESL student be a beginning student at one school and intermediate or advanced at another school?

Vocabulary

BUDDY: friend

ANYTHING TO WRITE HOME ABOUT: something interesting or exciting

TO SOCK AWAY A FEW BUCKS: to save some money

PLASTIC MONEY: credit cards

TO MAKE IT: to be on time; to get something done or go somewhere when you want to (in time); to earn money

ASSESSMENT: evaluation; appraisal

TO HOLD SOMEONE'S HAND: to be supportive; to offer friendship to someone who is worried about something

BIG ON SOMEONE'S LIST: enjoyable; something that is anticipated with pleasure

WEAK: the opposite of strong; lacking capability

TOEFL: Test of English as a Foreign Language

COUNSELOR: advisor

SUDDENLY: without warning

A PAIN: something you do not like to do; a person or thing that is boring, troublesome

PLACEMENT: to put in a particular position; to rank

NO KIDDING: really? is that true?

TO CONVINCE: to persuade; to cause someone to believe something

TO HANG AROUND: to stay in one place

A PIT STOP: a short stop on the way to somewhere else

TO CHECK SOMETHING OUT: to look into something; to investigate

THE ASSESSMENT TEST

Sharon: Hi Fred. How ya' doing?

Fred: Hey there, if it isn't my old chemistry buddy! It's good to see you back. Did ya' have a good summer?

Sharon: Well, I didn't do anything to write home about. How about you? Did ya' do anything exciting?

Fred: I managed to get up into the mountains for a few weeks, but I worked most of the summer. I've been trying to sock away a few bucks so I don't have to live on plastic money.

Sharon: Good for you. I usually spend my money faster than I can make it. What are you doing on campus so early? Classes don't begin for a few weeks yet.

Fred: My friend María Luz just flew in from Colombia last week, and she has to take the assessment test today. I promised to come down and hold her hand. She's pretty nervous.

Sharon: I don't blame her. Taking tests has never been big on my list of favorite things to do. Does your friend speak English pretty well?

Fred: Actually, she's a lawyer in Colombia, but she's still a little weak in English.

Sharon: Don't foreign students have to take a test before they can get into a school here?

Fred: Yeah, for most schools they have to take the TOEFL. María Luz took it in Colombia, and she did pretty well. But she's worried about her writing and speaking skills. That's what the assessment test is all about.

Sharon: Why does she have to take the assessment if she already took the TOEFL?

Fred: She asked the same question. The counselor said she needed the TOEFL test for admission as a student. The assessment is just to make sure she's put into the right level classes.

Sharon: Oh. That makes sense. But what if she came from another ESL program at another school?

Fred: She'd still have to take the assessment. The counselor said that because all programs are different, the levels are not the same.

Sharon: You mean a student could be in advanced classes at one school and in beginning classes at the other?

Fred: It's possible. Stranger things have happened. It doesn't mean that the student is suddenly not as smart or a lot smarter—it's just that the programs are different.

Sharon: Boy. That all sounds pretty complicated to me. I guess the assessment test is important. I don't like tests, but if they help me get into the right classes, they're worth the pain. Anyhow, it doesn't sound like the assessment is really a test; it sounds more like a placement.

Fred: You're right! That's just what it is. You know, even native English speakers have to take a writing assessment to get into English classes at most colleges.

Sharon: No kidding! Really?

Fred: Would I lie? Now all I have to do is to convince María Luz not to worry and just to do the best she can. Say, if you're just hanging around, why don't you come with me? We can make a pit stop for some coffee.

Sharon: I'll walk you as far as the bookstore. I want to get there early so I can find some of my textbooks used. They're a lot cheaper than new ones, so they go fast.

Fred: I should check them out, too. I'm not meeting María Luz until 11, and it's only 10:15 now.

Sharon: Oh boy! It's good to be back here at school!

Fred: Are you sick or something?

Sharon: No, just optimistic.

Postlistening/Reading Questions

| Answer in complete sentences. |

1. Where did Fred go during the summer?

   _____

2. Why is Fred on campus early?

   _____

3. Where is María Luz from?

   _____

4. What is she worried about?

   _____

5. Why does Sharon want to go to the bookstore early?

   _____

6. Why does María Luz need to take the assessment?

   _____

7. What kind of a job does María Luz have in Colombia?

   _____

8. How can an ESL student be a beginning student at one school and intermediate or advanced at another school?

   _____

Vocabulary Building Sentences

First, underline the word or expression from the vocabulary list in the prelistening/reading section. Then write a new sentence, using the same word or expression. Follow the model.

MODEL: Come on, loan me some money. I thought we were <u>buddies</u>!

Janet and David have been buddies for a long time.

1. Did you do anything last week to write home about?

2. I socked away some of the candy so I would have some to eat while I studied.

3. Plastic money can be dangerous. You always have to pay it back.

4. It seems like I will never be able to make it on time to catch the early bus.

5. Will you hold my hand? I have to go to the doctor and get a shot.

6. I just hung around the house all weekend.

7. Can we make a pit stop at the supermarket? I'm out of milk.

8. Hey, did you check out that new show on TV last night? It sure was boring.

9. I'm a little weak in history. Can you help me?

10. Making a lot of money has never been big on my list. I'd rather just be happy.

Word Forms

Complete the following sentences with the correct word form.

weak   weakest

1. I feel so _____. I haven't eaten since morning.

2. When it comes to chocolate, he is the _____ person I know.

assessment   assess   assessor

1. After she makes an _____ of the situation, she will make her decision.

2. He is the county tax _____.

3. The teacher can _____ your writing skills.

counsel   counselor   counseling

1. Did you take a _____ class last semester?

2. The priest will _____ the couple before they marry.

3. My _____ is very understanding.

placed   placement   place

1. Did you find a _____ to live?

2. Your _____ on the salary scale depends on how much experience you have had.

3. My brother _____ second in the race!

optimistic   optimist

1. An _____ says the glass is half full; the pessimist says it's half empty.

2. I'm very _____ about my classes this semester.

Conversation Activities

> Working in groups, discuss the following:

Why do you think many people are nervous about taking tests? Think about one test you had to take that made you nervous. What did you do to feel less nervous? Is it better for you to be by yourself when you are worried about an exam, or do you feel better with other people? Do you ever get together a study group with others taking the same exam? What would be better than testing that would show progress? In the United States, it is considered wrong to help a classmate when you are taking a test. Do you think this is right? What would you do if you saw someone cheating on a test?

Suggested Role-Plays

> Working in groups or in pairs, prepare a dialogue to share with the class. The following topics are suggestions for you to use.

1. **Participants: John and a school counselor**
   John has gone to the counselor's office to talk about his test results.

John:	Hello. Are you Ms. Brand?
Ms. Brand:	Yes, I am. You must be John. You're right on time for your appointment.
John:	Well, actually I'm a little nervous about the results of my English and math assessment tests. I've spoken English all my life. I didn't think I had to take tests to get in.
Ms. Brand:	The assessment isn't to get in. It's just to help us place you in the right level classes. We have several levels of both math and English, you know.
John:	Well, my parents told me to take the highest level English and math classes. They expect me to do very well.
Ms. Brand:	Let's take a look at the results of your assessment. Hmmmm . . . .

   Finish the dialogue.

2. **Participants: John, María Luz, Sharon, and Fred**
   Fred has taken María Luz to a pizza parlor to meet some of her new classmates.

Fred:	Well, here it is, María. It's not very exciting, but we like it. This is where we usually come when we need a break from studying for a while.
María Luz:	The pizza smells wonderful. I like the music.
Fred:	It gets pretty loud and crazy, but it's a lot of fun. Here are John and Sharon. They are the people I wanted you to meet.

   Finish the dialogue.

Listening Comprehension Cloze Passage

> Listen to the tape of the following passage or to your teacher. Fill in the missing words as you hear them.

Dear Mom and Dad,

Well, I've been here in the United States for _____ three
1

weeks now, and I miss you a _____ already. Everyone here is
2

very nice to me, and I _____ made many new friends. You
3

would like the place _____ I am living. I live with an American
4

family, _____ they all speak English to me all
5

the _____. I miss not speaking Spanish, and sometimes I get
6

_____, but I know the only way to learn a _____
7   8

is to use it all of the time. Sometimes my _____ hurts and I
9

want to hear Spanish _____ me! That _____ goes
10   11

away as soon as I go to school and get _____ with my new
12

friends.

I have a wonderful teacher for English. She has a lot of

_____ with me and has a good sense of _____,
13   14

too. She needs it with me as a student! There _____ a lot of
15

students from many different _____, so we all have to speak
16

English with each other. It's _____ different from when I was
17

studying English _____ Colombia where everyone spoke
18

Spanish. It seems _____ sometimes to hear English
19

_____ I go instead of Spanish. My teacher told me to try to do
20

lots of _____ in English, so I try to read the
21

_____ every day. It is difficult, but I think I am learning very
      22

_____.
      23

There is one other student here from Colombia, and

_____ we get together and _____ about home.
      24   25

She is from Bogotá. _____ we can come home for Christmas
                              26

_____. What would you think of that?
      27

Tell Jorge that I _____ have a new boyfriend and that I
                          28

miss _____ very much. Have some beans and arepas for
          29

_____.
      30

Your loving daughter,

María Luz

Final Project

1. Get out your dictionary and look up two words. The first is the word *optimist*. Write down the meaning of the word and use it in a sentence. Make sure that you understand it well. Now look up the word *pessimist*. Write down the meaning of the word and use it in a sentence. Make sure that you understand it well.
   Now you are ready to discuss your personal position. Are you an optimist or are you a pessimist? Explain why you call yourself one and not the other.

2. Talk about the differences between studying a language in the country where it is spoken as a first language, and where it is spoken as a foreign language. Where is it easier to learn? Why?

Glossary

A CITATION: a ticket; a piece of paper issued by a police officer that states what is wrong

A COUPLE OF BUCKS: a few dollars

A FINE: money paid as a penalty for doing something wrong or against the law

A GOOD DEAL: a good price or low price for something you buy

A LA CARTE: listed separately on the menu; not a complete meal

A LOAD: the quantity of clothes, towels, and so on that you put into a washing machine or dryer

A LOTTA STUFF: a lot of stuff; lots of possessions; many things

A MIDTERM: a test (examination) that is usually given in the middle of the semester or quarter

A MONSTER: a large machine

A PAIN: something you do not like to do; a person or thing that is boring, troublesome

A PIECE OF CAKE: it's easy

A PIT STOP: a short stop on the way to somewhere else

A PURIST: someone who believes everything should be in its pure or natural form

A REFUND: money returned to you

A RIP-OFF: a bad deal; a high price for something that should be less expensive

A SEC: a second; a very short period of time (This expression is common in fast, casual speech. When you are writing, it should always be written as *a second*.)

A SHOCK: a surprise, something unexpected (can be good or bad)

A STAR: a famous person in the world of entertainment; a way of ranking movies (one star is bad, two stars is fair, three stars is good, four stars is excellent)

A TOTAL SLOB: someone who is not careful about his or her appearance; someone who is not clean

ADDITIVES: chemicals and coloring added to food

ALL THAT JAZZ: and everything else

ANYTHING TO WRITE HOME ABOUT: something interesting or exciting

ARRANGE: to plan; to put in order

ASSESSMENT: evaluation; appraisal

AWFUL: terrible, very bad

BACK-TO-BACK: to have more than one thing to do with little or no time in between

BEFORE MY TIME: before I was born, before I knew about something or understood it

BIG ON SOMEONE'S LIST: enjoyable; something that is anticipated with pleasure

BLUE CHEESE DRESSING: salad dressing usually made of cheese, sour cream, mayonnaise, blue cheese, and spices

BOMB: something unsuccessful with the public (usually a movie, a play, or another kind of performance)

BRAINSTORM: a very good idea; usually an idea that comes like a storm—without warning or time to prepare for it

BRAVE: not afraid; strong and courageous

BUCKS: dollars

BUDDY: friend

BULLETIN BOARD: a special place or section on a wall where people are allowed to post notices advertising items for sale, services, housing, and so on

CHECKOUT STAND: the counter in a store where you pay for the things that you want to buy

CHEVY: Chevrolet—a popular make of American car

COULD'VE: could have (This pronunciation is common in fast, casual speech. In writing, it is *could have*.)

COUNSELOR: advisor

CRAZIES: crazy people; people who act strangely

CRITIC: someone who is paid to write about movies, plays, or art

CUTE: attractive, nice looking

DAIRY CASE: a glass case where dairy products are kept

DEEP-FRIED: cooked in a lot of oil or lard, usually in a deep pan

DELI: a delicatessen; a store that sells prepared food like sandwiches and salads

DENSE: thick, solid; crowded (population); stupid, slow to understand (a person)

DON'T GET ME WRONG: don't misunderstand me

DRIVING RECORD: the information stored in a computer at the Department of Motor Vehicles that says if you have been in accidents, have moving violations or parking tickets

D'YA: do you (This expression is common in fast, casual speech. When you are writing, these words should always be written as *do you*.)

DYNAMITE: something very good, great

D'YOU: do you (This is common in fast, casual speech. When you are writing, it should be written as *do you*.)

EASY COME, EASY GO: something you don't work hard to get is easy to spend or lose

'EM: them (This expression is common in fast, casual speech. When you are writing, it should be written as *them*.)

ENCOURAGE: to make someone feel better; to help someone feel he or she can do something

ESCARGOTS: a French word for small snails cooked in a sauce with white wine, butter, garlic, and parsley

EXPENSIVE: costing a lot of money; high in price; the opposite of *cheap*

EXPRESS LINE: a faster checkout stand where you can pay for your purchases if you have no more than a certain number of items

FADED: no longer bright and clear; old-looking

FANCY: decorated; ornate; not plain, not simple

FEATURE: showing; sometimes there are two features for one price (two movies)

FILM: movie

FIRMLY: strongly (but not too strongly)

FOOD STAMPS: stamps that are issued by the Federal government to low-income people. Food stamps can be used instead of money to buy food

FOXY: physically attractive; sexy

FRENCH DRESSING: salad dressing usually made with oil, vinegar, and spices

GLOVE COMPARTMENT: a small storage cabinet in the dashboard of an automobile

GONNA: going to (This is common in fast, casual speech. When you are writing, it should always be written as *going to*.)

GOTTA: (have) got to (This is common in fast, casual speech. When you are writing, it should be written as *got to*.)

GRAB A . . . :   to stop for a cup of coffee, soda, sandwich, quick meal, and so on

GROCERIES: meats, produce, dairy products, and household items

GRUMPY: to be unhappy or unpleasant

HEADLIGHT: a clear light mounted on each side of the front of a vehicle

HEAVY DUTY: serious, not frivolous

HERE WE GO AGAIN: when you recognize that you are saying or doing the same thing that you have said or done at an earlier time

HOPELESS: without hope; impossible to change or solve

HORROR: terror, fright, great fear; movies that are made intentionally to scare the audience

HOSTESS TWINKIES®:   a brand name for small, packaged cakes

HOT ON THE TRAIL OF: close to catching someone or something

HOUSE DRESSING: a specialty of a particular restaurant, not always the same

I'D: I would (This expression is common in fast, casual speech.)

I TOLD YOU SO: a reminder from someone that you didn't take his or her advice

I'LL HAVE YOU KNOW THAT: I want you to know that . . . (used for emphasis)

IN ONE PIECE: not damaged or harmed; safe and well

IN THE MEANTIME: for now; until something else happens

IT'D: it would (This is common in fast, casual speech. When you are writing, it should be written as *it would*.)

Glossary

IT'S THE SAME OLD STORY: when you recognize that you are hearing the same thing that you heard at an earlier time

JUST ISN'T YOUR NIGHT (OR DAY): this is a bad time for you; you are not lucky right now

JUNK: something that has no value to someone

MA'AM: a contraction of *madam*; commonly used as a polite manner of address to a woman who is older than you are (Note: *Ma'am* is a more common manner of address in Southern dialects than in Northern dialects of American English.)

MATINEE: an afternoon showing (sometimes less expensive)

MENU: a written list of food, drinks, and prices in a restaurant

MUNCHIES: any small things (like fruit, potato chips, cookies) that are good to eat (to munch on); not a full meal; snacks

NAH: no (This expression is common in fast, casual speech. When you are writing, it should be written as *no*.)

NEVER TOUCH THE STUFF: never eat or drink something

NO KIDDING: really? is that true?

NO WAY: (slang) impossible

NOT TO WORRY: don't worry

NOTHING TO SNEEZE AT: something that is important; something that has more significance than it is given

OCTOPUS: a sea animal which has eight tentacles

OFFHAND: something that comes into your mind casually; without careful thought or consideration

ORGANIC: natural, produced without chemicals or additives

OUT OF LUCK: unlucky

OUT OF MY LEAGUE: something you are not accustomed to; something that often feels too sophisticated, advanced, or difficult

OUTRAGEOUS: something that is either very good or very bad

PERK: a bonus; something good that is unexpected (This term is commonly used to describe extra employee benefits.)

PERMANENT DAMAGE: harm that is impossible to fix; harm that is beyond repair

PLACEMENT: to put in a particular position; to rank

PLASTIC MONEY: credit cards

PLOT: the story line in a play, movie, or book

POLITE: courteous, well-mannered, considerate of others

POSITIVELY: definitely; without a doubt

POTLUCK: a meal made from whatever is available or contributed by others

PRETTY SURE: reasonably sure of something

PREVIEWS: short films that are advertisements for movies that will play at that theater the future (also called *trailers*)

PROOF: information that shows something is true; evidence

PSYCH: abbreviation for psychology; the science of mind and behavior

R AND R: Rest and relaxation; something relaxing, enjoyable (Originally a military term, R and R has become quite common in casual speech.)

RED SNAPPER: a kind of ocean fish especially popular, as food, on the West Coast

REFUND: money returned to you

REMODELING: fixing something up; changing something to make it better, newer, more convenient

REVIEW: a short critical article or discussion

RIGHT UP ONE'S ALLEY: what one likes to do, or does well

ROWDY: noisy and often uncontrolled; not reserved

RUNNING (SOMEONE AROUND): to drive someone where he or she needs to go (This expression is common in casual speech.)

SCREEN: the large white area on which movies are shown

SENSIBLE: showing clear thinking; practical; of good judgment

SHELL: a hard or tough outer covering; a framework or exterior cover

SHOOT: go ahead; say what you want to say; used in conversation to mean "ask me" or "tell me"

SHOPPING CART: a metal basket with wheels for carrying groceries

SLIMY: covered with a mucous secretion; slippery

SPUR OF THE MOMENT: without forethought; a decision to do something that has not been carefully planned or prearranged

STEREOTYPE: seeing all people of a particular sex, race, or religion as the same

STINKY: something that is offensive or that doesn't smell good (This expression is used in casual speech among people of the same age.)

SUBTITLES: translated dialogue at the bottom of the screen in foreign films

SUDDENLY: without warning

TAIL LIGHT: a red warning light mounted on each side of the back of a vehicle

TAKE IT EASY: relax; calm down; don't worry; be happy

TEN TO: ten minutes before the hour

TENTACLES: long, spider-like arms

THAT'D: that would (This pronunciation is common in fast, casual speech. When you're writing, it should be written as *that would*.)

THE PITS: unpleasant; boring; something you don't like to do

THERE'RE: there are (This expression is common fast, casual speech. When you are writing, it should be written as *there are*.)

THEY'D: they would (This pronunciation is common in fast, casual speech. When you are writing, it should be written as *they would*.)

THOUSAND ISLAND DRESSING: salad dressing usually made of mayonnaise, tomato sauce, pickles, spices, and chopped hard-cooked eggs

TO ACE (a test or a course): to do very well; to get an excellent grade

TO BAIL SOMEONE OUT: to help someone when he or she is in trouble; often to help financially or emotionally; to give money to release someone from jail

TO BE ABLE TO HANDLE (SOMETHING OR SOMEONE): to be able to tolerate or to deal with someone or something

TO BE ALL SET: to be ready to do something; to be prepared for something

TO BE ALL SETTLED: to arrange something; to take care of something so it is no longer a problem

TO BE BALD: not to have hair on your head; not to have tread on tires

TO BE GOING ON: to be happening; occurring

TO BE GRATEFUL: to be full of thanks; to appreciate someone or something

TO BE HARD ON SOMEONE: to be strict with; to be difficult

TO BE KIDDING: to be pretending, joking, fooling

TO BE LIBERATED: to be aware of your rights as a person

TO BE OFF (SOMEONE'S) LIST: to give up on something or someone; to decide something or someone is not worth the trouble to deal with

TO BE ON A ROLL: to have things going smoothly; to build up momentum; to be moving physically or mentally

TO BE ON SALE: to be at a lower price; to be cheaper than usual

TO BE ON THE SAFE SIDE: to be careful; to protect yourself

TO BE OUT OF LINE: to do or say something that is inappropriate or wrong

TO BE RIDICULOUS: to be foolish; to be silly

TO BE TIGHT ABOUT SOMETHING: to be strict; to be conservative with money

TO BE USED TO: to be accustomed to something

TO BE WORTH A SHOT: to be worth a try; to have enough value to warrant an effort

TO BE WORTH SAVING: to be something that still has some value; to be something that you should not throw away

TO BREAK A DOLLAR BILL: to make change; to spend part of

TO BREAK EVEN: to make as much money as you spend; to neither lose nor win something; to end up with the same amount you started with

TO CATCH ON: to understand what's happening, to comprehend suddenly

TO CHECK (SOMETHING OR SOMEONE) OUT: to look at, to study, to evaluate

TO CHECK A LIST: to refer to a piece of paper where you have written down the things you need

TO CHECK INTO: to study something, to look into something

TO CHECK OUT: to look at something; to leave (check out of a hotel or motel; to pay fo[r] your purchases at a cashier's counter)

TO CHECK (SOMETHING OR SOMEONE) OUT: to look into something; to investigate; to study; to evaluate

TO CHICKEN OUT: to decide not to do something because you are afraid of doing it

TO CHILL OUT: to relax; to calm down; to become less serious

TO CLEAN UP: to make a lot of money

TO COME ON TOO STRONG: to present yourself in a forceful way; to push yourself on someone

TO CONNECT WITH: to meet; to contact; to get together with

TO CONVINCE: to persuade; to cause someone to believe something

TO CUT IN FRONT OF: to move or to push your way in front of someone or something

TO CUT IT OUT: to stop talking

TO DEAL WITH (SOMETHING OR SOMEONE):   to take care of, to handle, to resolve

TO DISCRIMINATE: to prefer one group of people more than another group of people

TO DRAG SOMEONE SOMEWHERE: to take someone somewhere he or she really doesn't want to go

TO DROP OUT OF: to stop attending an activity; to stop belonging to a group

TO END UP (ORDERING):   what you finally have or decide to have; what you are left with

TO END UP DOING SOMETHING: to do something you did not plan (or want) to do

TO EXPECT: to think that something is going to happen; to wait for something you expect will come

TO FEEL FUNNY: to feel strange; to feel awkward

TO FIX: to make or prepare (food); to repair

TO FORK OUT BIG BUCKS: to spend a lot of money

TO GET (IT, SOMETHING) OUT OF THE WAY: to finish something; to complete it; to put something aside

TO GET CARRIED AWAY: to become involved in what you are doing (often so much that you forget other things)

TO GET DOWN TO: to get to the heart (of something); to the important part (This expression is common in many situations and people of different age groups—for example, "Let's get down to business.")

TO GET DOWN TO NOTHING: to have nothing left that is clean to wear; to have nothing left to eat; to have no money left to spend

TO GET SOMETHING OVER WITH: to finish something that you don't want to do

TO GET SOMEWHERE: to accomplish something, to be successful

TO GET THROUGH: to finish; to complete

TO GET TO BE: to become

TO GET UP THE COURAGE: to become brave enough to do something that is difficult

TO GIVE SOMEONE A BREAK: to give someone a chance; to make things easier for that person

TO GIVE SOMEONE A CALL: to call someone on the telephone

TO GIVE SOMEONE A LIFT: to give someone a ride in a car

TO GIVE SOMETHING A TRY: to try something; to make an attempt at a job, a lesson, and so on

TO GO BROKE: to spend or use all of your money

TO GO DUTCH: each person pays for his or her share of the bill

TO GO RIGHT AWAY: to sell or rent quickly

TO GO UP (in price): to become more expensive

TO GRIPE: to express pain, unhappiness, or displeasure

TO HANDLE (SOMETHING OR SOMEONE): to take care of, to deal with, to resolve

TO HANG AROUND: to stay in one place

TO HAVE COURAGE: to be brave; to have strength

TO HAVE GOOD EARS: to be a good listener

TO HAVE SOMEONE'S NUMBER: to understand someone; to have him or her figured out; to know a person's likes or dislikes

TO HESITATE: to wait before you do or say something

TO HIT IT (RIGHT ON THE HEAD): to arrive at a specific time or place; to concentrate or focus on something; to get something done

TO HOLD SOMEONE'S HAND: to be supportive; to offer friendship to someone who is worried about something

TO JUMP RIGHT OUT AT: to be very noticeable; to be obvious

TO KEEP AN EYE ON: to watch

TO KEEP UP (WITH THE JONESES): to continue; to go at the same speed as others

TO KICK BACK: to relax; to take it easy

TO KNOW WHAT SOMETHING IS LIKE: to understand; to be sympathetic to someone

TO LIGHTEN UP: become less serious; to relax

TO LIVE AND LEARN: to learn more as you get older

TO MAKE IT: to be on time; to get something done or go somewhere when you want to (in time); to earn money

TO MAKE RESERVATIONS: to make arrangements ahead of time; to telephone the place you are going to in advance in order to set a specific time for you to arrive

TO MIND (SOMETHING): to object to; to be mildly against something

TO MIX AND MATCH: to try different combinations; to put things together

TO PACK UP: to put things away; to get ready to go

TO PART WITH (SOMETHING OR SOMEONE): to give something up; to relinqu[i]
something; to let someone go

TO PARTY: common noun that has recently gained acceptance as a verb; it is conjugated a[s]
a regular verb

TO PASS: to choose not to do something; to let something go by

TO PAY ATTENTION TO: to notice

TO PICK (SOMEONE OR SOMETHING) UP: to take on or away; to receive, to get; to pay
for someone else (to pick up the check)

TO PRESENT A GOOD IMAGE: to make people think well of you; to make a good impression

TO PUT OFF (doing something): to avoid; to postpone

TO PUT SOMETHING MILDLY: to understate something; to make something sound less
serious than it is

TO RAKE IT IN: to make a lot of money (A mint is a place where the government takes paper and metals to produce currency and coins.)

TO REJECT: to push someone or something away; to refuse

TO RUN OUT OF: not to have any more of something

TO SET THINGS (SOMETHING) UP: to prepare, to organize

TO SHIFT AROUND: to change positions; not to sit still in your seat

TO SHOW SOMEONE AROUND: to help make someone feel more comfortable by helping
them learn about something

TO SHOW UP: to come; to appear; to arrive

TO SIGN OFF: to approve something with an official signature; to say goodnight or goodbye

TO SLAVE OVER A HOT STOVE: to work hard cooking something

TO SOCK AWAY A FEW BUCKS: to save some money

TO STARE: to look at steadily without looking away

TO STARVE: to be very, very hungry; to be without food

TO STOCK UP: to get a lot of something at one time

TO STRETCH SOMETHING OUT: to add other things so that something will last longer,
go farther, or feed more people

TO STRUGGLE THROUGH: to fight with; to work very hard for or at something

TO TAKE A BREAK: to stop doing something for a period of time; to rest

TO TAKE A LOOK AT: to investigate; to consider; to examine something

TO TAKE A RISK: to take a chance; to do something that may not be completely safe

TO TAKE DOWN: to write; to note something

TO TAKE IN: to go see; to look at

TO TAKE OFF: to leave

TO THROW TOGETHER: to make in a hurry, often without care

TO TOSS SOMETHING OUT: to throw something away

TO TRANSFER: to send from one person or place to another

TO TURN INTO: to become or change

TO WORK OUT: to happen to someone's advantage; to happen the way you want something to happen

TOEFL: Test of English as a Foreign Language

TOUGH: difficult; unfortunate

TRAFFIC: movement of cars, buses, trucks, ships, planes, or other vehicles in or through a certain area

TRANS AM: an American-made fast car

TRASHY: cheap; something that has no significant value

UTILITIES: services like electricity, heat, and water often provided by public companies

VEGETARIAN: a person who does not eat meat

VEGGIES: vegetables

WAGES: money earned by working

WANNA: want to (This expression is common in fast, casual speech. When you are writing, it should be written as *want to*.)

WANT ADS: newspaper advertisements saying something or someone is wanted

WE'VE: we have (This is common in fast, casual speech. When you are writing, it should be written as *we have*.)

WEAK: the opposite of strong; lacking capability

WEIRD: strange; unusual; unexplainable; disturbing

WHADDAYA WANT: what do you want?

WHADDAYA: what do you

WHAT'D: what did (This is common in fast, casual speech. When you are writing, it should be written as *what did*.)

WHERE'S: where is (This is common in fast, casual speech. When you are writing, it should be written as *where is*.)

WHOA: wait a minute (This expression is common only in casual speech.)

WINNER: something or someone successful

YA': you (This expression is common in fast, casual speech. When you are writing, it should be written as *you*.)

YEAH: yes (This expression is common in fast, casual speech. When you are writing, it should always be written as *yes*.)

YELLOW PAGES: the part of the telephone book which has advertisements for businesses and services

YOU'D: you would (This expression is common in fast, casual speech. In writing, it shou
be *you would*.)

YUCK: a common expression of dislike

YUP: yes (This is common in fast, casual speech. When you are writing, it should be written
as *yes*.)